love stitches™

General Information

Many of the products used in this pattern book can be purchased from local craft, fabric and variety stores, or from the Annie's Attic Needlecraft Catalog (see Customer Service information on page 64).

Contents

Charities

Crocheters have nimble fingers and large hearts. Their talents provide warmth to the needy, a cheery welcome to the newborn and comfort to the dispossessed. Their handmade gifts remind a patriot of a nation's gratitude, and a troubled child that someone cares. Their crocheting skills encircle the world, covering it with loving stitches.

We have assembled a collection of charities that accept crocheted articles and distribute them where they are needed, and a diverse collection of practical items suitable for donating to those charities. Every little stitch helps; every little act of kindness makes the world a better place.

LOVE STITCHES FOR CHILDREN
Binky Patrol

Binky Patrol is 100% volunteer. They deliver handmade blankets to shelters, hospitals and any child or teen in need of comfort or a reminder that someone cares. "All sizes of blankets are needed. They accept any pattern as long as it is soft, washable and comes from your heart." Official chapters are listed on **www.binkypatrol.org**.

Project Linus

"Project Linus is a nonprofit organization with a twofold mission.

First, it is our mission to provide love, a sense of security, warmth and comfort to children who are seriously ill, traumatized or otherwise in need through the gifts of new, handmade blankets and afghans, lovingly created by volunteer 'blanketeers.'

Second, it is our mission to provide a rewarding and fun service opportunity for interested individuals and groups in local communities, for the benefit of children." To find out more about Project Linus go to:

www.projectlinus.org
or contact them at:
Project Linus National Headquarters,
P.O. Box 5621, Bloomington, IL 61702-5621
(309) 454-1764

Stitches from the Heart

"Stitches from the Heart is a nonprofit organization that sends handmade clothing, blankets and love to premature babies all across the nation. We also have a senior program that helps seniors help others by donating yarn and supplies. We are located in Santa Monica, Calif. If you want to help, but are unable to devote the time to knit, crochet or quilt, you can make a much needed financial contribution." Send contributions to:

Stitches from the Heart, 3316 Pico Blvd.,
Santa Monica, CA 90405

LOVE STITCHES FOR CHARITIES
Hospice

Hospice exists to help those who cope personally or professionally with terminal illness, death and the process of grief and bereavement. Hospice staff and volunteers provide comfort and support to patients and their families. As an act of kindness, you can give a handmade gift to a patient or a family member. To locate a hospice near you, go to **www.hospicedirectory.org**

Heart Awareness

The American Heart Association provides programs to educate people about the effects of cardiovascular disease and strokes. Wearing red is a way to raise awareness of the issues of women and heart disease. Information on how to organize a Wear Red event in your community is posted on their Web site, **www.americanheart.org**.

Cancer Awareness

Many cancer patients face the heartwrenching side effect of chemotherapy hair loss during treatments meant to help them recover. Not only must these cancer patients face a life-threatening illness, they must also learn to deal with seeing a different person in the mirror. Wearing a handmade cap can help patients feel like themselves again and lets them know that someone cares. When crocheting chemo hats remember softer yarns like cotton are more comfortable to sensitive heads. Do not use wool or fabric softeners as many people are allergic to them. To donate your chemotherapy hats to the patients that need them, look in your phone book to find hospitals or cancer organizations in your area and give them a call to see if they are accepting cancer hat donations.

LOVE STITCHES FOR MILITARY
Soldiers' Angels

Soldiers' Angels is a volunteer-led, nonprofit organization providing aid and comfort to the men and women of the United States Army, Marines, Navy, Air Force, Coast Guard and their families. Founded by the mother of two American soldiers, we are an international volunteer-led organization supporting America's men and women in uniform. With over 30 different teams and projects, our nearly 200,000 volunteers assist veterans, wounded and deployed personnel and their families in a variety of unique and effective ways." To find out more about this organization go to **www.soldiersangels.org**

HAP

The objective of Handmade Afghans Project (HAP) "is to thank those who were wounded in service to our country. To bring comfort and warmth to our wounded service members, we create handmade afghans. The afghans are sent to ten military hospitals including Walter Reed A.M.C. in Washington, D.C., Landstuhl Regional Hospital in Germany and Craig Joint Theater Hospital in Afghanistan. You can help by crocheting or knitting 6" x 9" rectangles that will be joined with rectangles made by others to produce twin bed-size afghans." To learn more about this organization, go to their Web site at **www.rectangle6x9.org**

LOVE STITCHES FOR ANIMALS
Hugs for Homeless Animals

Hugs for Homeless Animals is a multiservice, nonprofit organization dedicated to helping homeless and displaced animals worldwide. They ask for donations of handmade blankets to local humane societies and animal shelters. The blankets can be crocheted, knitted or sewn in the following guideline sizes: 14 x 14 inches (small), 24 x 24 inches (medium) and 36 x 36 inches (large). They may be cotton or acrylic in any color and should not have fringe that animals can chew off and swallow.

For more information about the Hugs for Homeless Animals organization, visit their Web site at **www.h4ha.org**.

LOVE STITCHES FOR THE DISPLACED
Hats for the Homeless

Hats for the Homeless began with one young man's desire to care about those less fortunate. He died suddenly in 1998, and the organization was created in his memory to continue the tradition he started. Through Hats for the Homeless, hats, scarves and gloves are collected throughout the year, gift-wrapped and distributed to a large population of urban homeless. If you would like to participate, crochet, knit or just buy a hat, scarf or pair of gloves, and send it to the following address:

Hats for the Homeless 905 Main St., Hackensack, NJ 07601 **info@hats4thehomeless.org**

Warm Up America! Foundation

Sponsored by the Craft Yarn Council of America (CYCA), Warm Up America! is an organization that is dedicated to keeping people in need warm with handmade afghans and blankets. They ask for volunteers, working together with family, friends or groups to crochet or knit 7 x 9-inch sections, assemble them into afghans and distribute them to needy recipients in their own communities. When this is not possible, the CYCA will gladly accept donations of both individual sections or strips needing assembly and completed afghans. For more information on the Warm Up America project, visit their website at **www.warmupamerica.com**

Donated items should be sent to Warm Up America! Foundation, 469 Hospital Drive, 2nd Floor Suite E, Gastonia, NC 28054.

love stitches
for Children

CAPS **for Kids**

CLUSTER & SHELL HAT
DESIGN BY **SUE CHILDRESS**

SKILL LEVEL

INTERMEDIATE

FINISHED SIZE
Girl's size

MATERIALS
- Medium (worsted) weight yarn:
  3½ oz/175 yds/85g red
- Size F/5/3.75mm crochet hook or
  size needed to obtain gauge

MEDIUM

GAUGE
1 shell = 1 inch

PATTERN NOTES
For smaller Hat, use sport weight yarn.

Chain-3 at beginning of row or round counts as
first double crochet unless otherwise stated.

Chain-4 at beginning of row or round counts
as first double crochet and chain-1 unless
otherwise stated.

Join with slip stitch as indicated unless
otherwise stated.

SPECIAL STITCHES
Beginning cluster (beg cl): Ch 3, holding back last
lp of each st on hook, 3 dc in place indicated,
yo, pull through all lps on hook, ch 1.

Cluster (cl): Holding back last lp of each st on
hook, 4 dc in place indicated, yo, pull through
all lps on hook, ch 1.

Beginning shell (beg shell): Ch 3, (dc, ch 2, 2 dc)
in same place.

Shell: (2 dc, ch 2, 2 dc) in place indicated.

INSTRUCTIONS
HAT

Rnd 1: Ch 6, sl st in first ch to form ring, **ch 3** *(see Pattern Notes)*, 13 dc in ring, **join** *(see Pattern Notes)* in 3rd ch of beg ch-3. *(14 dc)*

Rnd 2: Sl st in next st, **ch 4** *(see Pattern Notes)*, **cl** *(see Special Stitches)* in next st, [ch 1, dc in next st, ch 1, cl in next st] around, ch 1, join in 3rd ch of beg ch-4. *(14 ch sps)*

Rnd 3: Ch 3, 3 dc in next ch sp, 4 dc in each ch sp around, join in 3rd ch of beg ch-3. *(56 dc)*

Rnd 4: Sl st in next st, ch 4, cl in next st, [sk next st, dc in next st, ch 1, cl in next st] around, join in 3rd ch of beg ch-4.

Rnd 5: Sl st in first ch sp, ch 3, dc in same ch sp, 2 dc in each ch sp around, join in 3rd ch of beg ch-3. *(76 dc)*

Rnd 6: Sl st in next st, **beg shell** *(see Special Stitches)* in same st, [sk next 3 sts, **shell** *(see Special Stitches)* in next st] around, sk last 3 sts, join in 3rd ch of beg ch-3. *(19 shells)*

Rnds 7–9: Sl st across to first ch sp, sl st in ch sp, beg shell in same ch sp, shell in ch sp of each shell around, join in 3rd ch of beg ch-3.

Rnd 10: Sl st across to first ch sp, sl st in first ch sp, **beg cl** *(see Special Stitches)* in same ch sp, dc in sp between shell, [ch 1, cl in ch sp of next shell, dc in sp between shells] around, ch 1, join in 3rd ch of beg ch-3. *(38 ch sps)*

Rnd 11: Sl st in first ch sp, ch 3, 2 dc in same ch sp, dc in next ch sp, [2 dc in next ch sp, dc in next ch sp] around, join in 3rd ch of beg ch-3. *(58 dc)*

Rnd 12: Ch 3, dc in each st around, join in 3rd ch of beg ch-3.

Rnd 13: Ch 1, 2 sc in first st, sc in each of next 28 sts, 2 sc in next st, sc in each rem st around, join in beg sc. *(60 sc)*

Rnd 14: Ch 1, sc in first st, *sk next 2 sts, 5 dc in next st, sk next 2 sts**, sc in next st, rep from * around, ending last rep at **, join in beg sc. Fasten off.

POST STITCH HAT
DESIGN BY **SUE CHILDRESS**

SKILL LEVEL

INTERMEDIATE

FINISHED SIZE
Boy's one size fits most

MATERIALS
- Patons Canadiana medium (worsted) weight yarn (3½ oz/ 241 yds/100g per ball):
  1 ball #00032 bright royal blue
- Size F/5/3.75mm crochet hook or size needed to obtain gauge

GAUGE
4 dc = 1 inch

PATTERN NOTES
For smaller hat, use light (light worsted) weight yarn: 1¾ oz/191/50g red.

Chain-2 at beginning of row or round counts as first half double crochet unless otherwise stated.

Chain-3 at beginning of row or round counts as first double crochet unless otherwise stated.

Join with slip stitch as indicated unless otherwise stated.

INSTRUCTIONS
HAT

Rnd 1: Ch 6, sl st in first ch to form ring, **ch 2** *(see Pattern Notes)*, 15 hdc in ring, **join** *(see Pattern Notes)* in 2nd ch of beg ch-2. *(16 hdc)*

Rnd 2: Sl st in next st, **ch 3** *(see Pattern Notes)*, dc in same st, 2 dc in each st around, join in 3rd ch of beg ch-3. *(32 dc)*

Rnd 3: Sl st in next st, ch 3, dc in same st, dc in next st, [2 dc in next st, dc in next st] around, join in 3rd ch of beg ch-3. *(48 dc)*

Rnd 4: Sl st in next st, ch 3, dc in next st, 2 dc in next st, [dc in each of next 2 sts, 2 dc in next st] around, join in 3rd ch of beg ch-3. *(64 dc)*

Rnd 5: Ch 3, dc in each of next 2 sts, 2 **fpdc** *(see Stitch Guide)* around next st, [dc in each of next 3 sts, 2 fpdc around next st] around. *(80 sts)*

Rnds 6 & 7: Ch 3, dc in each of next 2 sts, fpdc around each of next 2 fpdc, [dc in each of next 3 sts, fpdc around each of next 2 fpdc] around, join in 3rd ch of beg ch-3.

Rnds 8–12: Ch 3, fpdc around next st, dc in next st, fpdc around each of next 2 fpdc, [dc in next st, fpdc around next st, dc in next st, fpdc around each of next 2 fpdc] around, join in 3rd ch of beg ch-3.

Rnd 13: Ch 3, dc in each of next 2 sts, **dc dec** *(see Stitch Guide)* in next 2 sts, [dc in each of next 3 sts, dc dec in next 2 sts] around, join in 3rd ch of beg ch-3. *(64 dc)*

Rnd 14: Ch 3, dc in each st around, join in 3rd ch of beg ch-3.

Rnd 15: Ch 3, fpdc around next st, **bpdc** *(see Stitch Guide)* around each of next 2 sts, [fpdc around each of next 2 sts, bpdc around each of next 2 sts] around, join in 3rd ch of beg ch-3.

Rnd 16: Ch 1, sc in each st around, join in beg sc. Fasten off.

RIBBED HAT
DESIGN BY **ALINE SUPLINSKAS**

SKILL LEVEL

BEGINNER

FINISHED SIZES
Instructions given fit child's size 4–8 (small/medium); for larger size use size I/9/5mm or size J/10/6mm crochet hook

MATERIALS
- Red Heart Super Saver medium (worsted) weight yarn (5 oz/244 yds/141g per skein):
  1 skein #950 Mexicana
- Size H/8/5mm crochet hook or size needed to obtain gauge
- Tapestry needle

GAUGE
Size H hook: 4 sc = inch; 4 sc rows = 1 inch

PATTERN NOTES
Hat is worked vertically.

Join with slip stitch as indicated unless otherwise stated.

INSTRUCTIONS
HAT
Row 1: Ch 39, sc in 2nd ch from hook, sc in each ch across, turn. *(38 sc)*

Row 2: Ch 1, working in **back lps** *(see Stitch Guide)*, sc in each of first 37 sc, leaving last sc unworked at top of Hat, turn. *(37 sc)*

Row 3: Working in back lps, ch 1, sc in each st across, turn.

Row 4: Ch 1, working in back lps, sc in each of first 37 sts, sc in sk sc 3 rows below, turn. *(38 sc)*

Row 5: Ch 1, working in back lps, sc in each st across, turn.

Rows 6–65: [Rep rows 2–5 consecutively] 15 times.

Row 66: Fold opposite side of foundation ch to row 65 and working through both thicknesses, ch 1, sc in each st across. Fasten off.

Weave a length of yarn through sps at top of Hat created by working 37 sts, pull ends tight to close. Secure yarn. ■

Simple Shells Blanket
DESIGN BY CINDY ADAMS

SKILL LEVEL

INTERMEDIATE

FINISHED SIZE
33 x 34 inches

MATERIALS
- Medium (worsted) weight yarn:
  10 oz/500 yds/284g lavender
- Size G/6/4mm crochet hook or size
  needed to obtain gauge

4 MEDIUM

GAUGE
5 dc group = 1 inch

PATTERN NOTES
Chain-3 at beginning of row or round counts as
  first double crochet unless otherwise stated.

Join with slip stitch as indicated unless
  otherwise stated.

INSTRUCTIONS
AFGHAN
Row 1: Ch 126, sc in 2nd ch from hook and in
  each ch across, turn. *(125 sc)*

Row 2 (RS): Ch 3 *(see Pattern Notes)*, sk next
  st, *5 dc in next st**, sk next 3 sts, rep from *
  across, ending last rep at **, sk next st, dc in last
  st, turn.

Row 3: Ch 1, sc in first st, ch 2, sc in center dc of
  next dc group, [ch 3, sc in center dc of next dc
  group] across, ch 2, sc in last st, turn.

Row 4: Ch 3, 5 dc in each sc across, ending with
  dc in last st, turn.

Next rows: Rep rows 3 and 4 until piece
  measures 32 inches.

EDGING
Rnd 1: Working around outer edge in sts, ends of
  rows and in starting ch on opposite side of row
  1, ch 1, sc in first st, ch 2, (sc, ch 3) in center of
  each dc group and in end of each sc row around
  with ch 2 before and after each corner across
  each short edge and with (sc, ch 3, sc) in each
  corner, **join** *(see Pattern Notes)* in beg sc, turn.

Rnd 2: Sl st in last ch sp, ch 3, 4 dc in same ch sp
  at corner, *5 dc in each sc across** to ch-2 sp
  before corner, sk next sc, 5 dc in corner ch-3 sp,
  5 dc in next sc, rep from * around, ending last
  rep at **, join in 3rd ch of beg ch-3. Fasten off. ■

Receiving
Blanket & Booties

DESIGN BY **SUE CHILDRESS**

BABY BOOTIES
SKILL LEVEL

INTERMEDIATE

FINISHED SIZE

3½-inch sole

MATERIALS

- Red Heart Designer Sport light (light worsted) weight yarn (3 oz/ 279 yds/85g per ball):
    1 ball #3215 lemon zest
- Size F/5/3.75mm crochet hook or size needed to obtain gauge
- ⅜-inch ribbon: 1 yd

GAUGE

4 dc = 1 inch

PATTERN NOTES

Chain-2 at beginning of row or round counts as first half double crochet unless otherwise stated.

Chain-3 at beginning of row or round counts as first double crochet unless otherwise stated.

Join with slip stitch as indicated unless otherwise stated.

INSTRUCTIONS
BOOTIE
MAKE 2.

Rnd 1: Ch 11, 2 hdc in 3rd ch from hook (*first 2 chs count as first hdc*), hdc in each of next 7 chs, 3 dc in last ch, working on opposite side of ch, hdc in each of next 8 chs, **join** (*see Pattern Notes*) in 2nd ch of beg ch-2. (*21 sts*)

Rnd 2: **Ch 2** (*see Pattern Notes*), 2 hdc in each of next 2 sts, sc in each of next 6 sts, 2 hdc in next st, 2 dc in each of next 2 sts, 2 hdc in next st, sc in each of last 8 sts, 2 hdc in same st as beg ch-2, join in 2nd ch of beg ch-2. (*29 sts*)

Rnd 3: Ch 2, 2 hdc in next st, hdc in each of next 3 sts, sc in each of next 7 sts, hdc in next st, (hdc, dc) in next st, 2 dc in each of next 3 sts, (dc, hdc) in next st, sc in each of next 9 sts, 2 hdc in next st, hdc in last st, join in 2nd ch of beg ch-2. (*36 sts*)

Rnd 4: Ch 2, **bphdc** (*see Stitch Guide*) around each st around, join in 2nd ch of beg ch-2.

Rnd 5: Ch 2, hdc in each of next 14 sts, [**dc dec** (*see Stitch Guide*) in next 2 sts] 3 times, hdc in each rem st around, join in 2nd ch of beg ch-2. (*33 sts*)

Rnd 6: Ch 2, hdc in each of next 12 sts, [dc dec in next 2 sts] 3 times, hdc in each rem st around, join in 2nd ch of beg ch-2. *(30 sts)*

Rnd 7: Ch 2, **hdc dec** *(see Stitch Guide)* in next 2 sts, hdc in each of next 9 sts, [dc dec in next 2 sts] twice, hdc in each rem st around, join in 2nd ch of beg ch-2. *(27 sts)*

Rnd 8 (eyelet): Ch 4 *(counts as first dc and ch-1)*, sk next st, dc in next st, [ch 1, sk next st, dc in next st] around, ch 1, join in 3rd ch of beg ch-4. *(14 ch sps)*

Rnd 9: Ch 3 *(see Pattern Notes)*, 2 dc in same ch sp, sc in next ch sp, [3 dc in next ch sp, sc in next ch sp] around, join in 3rd ch of beg ch-3. Fasten off.

Weave 18-inch piece of ribbon through ch sps on rnd 8 beg and ending in front.

RECEIVING BLANKET
SKILL LEVEL

INTERMEDIATE

FINISHED SIZE
27 inches square

MATERIALS
- Bernat Baby Jacquards light (light worsted) weight yarn (3½ oz/ 346 yds/100g per ball):
  2 balls #06615 lemon pie
- Size F/5/3.75mm crochet hook or size needed to obtain gauge

GAUGE
4 dc = 1 inch; 3 rows = 1¾ inches

PATTERN NOTE
Chain-3 at beginning of row or round counts as first double crochet unless otherwise stated.

SPECIAL STITCH
Cluster (cl): Holding back last lp of each st on hook, 3 dc in place indicated, yo, pull through all sts on hook.

INSTRUCTIONS
BLANKET
Row 1: Ch 104, dc in 4th ch from hook, [**dc dec** *(see Stitch Guide)* in next 2 chs] twice, *[ch 1, **cl** *(see Special Stitch)* in next ch] 5 times, ch 1**, [dc dec in next 2 sts] 6 times, rep from * across to last 6 sts, ending last rep at **, [dc dec in next 2 chs] 3 times, turn.

Row 2: **Ch 3** *(see Pattern Note)*, dc in same st, dc in each st and in each ch across, leaving turning ch unworked, turn. *(102 dc)*

Row 3: Ch 3, dc in next st, [dc dec in next 2 sts] twice, *[ch 1, cl in next st] 5 times, ch 1**, [dc dec in next 2 sts] 6 times, rep from * across to last 6 sts, ending last rep at **, [dc dec in next 2 sts] 3 times, turn.

Next rows: [Rep rows 2 and 3 alternately] 22 times or until piece measures 27 inches. At end of last row, **do not turn.**

EDGING
Working around outer edge, ch 1, 3 hdc in end of first row, [2 hdc in end of next row, 3 hdc in end of next row] across, working in starting ch on opposite side of row 1, 3 sc in first ch, sc in each ch across with 3 sc in last ch, 3 hdc in end of first row, [2 hdc in end of next row, 3 hdc in end of next row] across, 3 sc in first st, sc in each st and ch across with 3 sc in last st, join with sl st in beg hdc. Fasten off. ∎

Froggy
Security Blanket

DESIGN BY **HELEN RICHARDSON HEAVERIN**

SKILL LEVEL
◧■▭▭
EASY

FINISHED SIZE
10 inches square, excluding trim

MATERIALS
- Caron Simply Soft Brites medium (worsted) weight yarn (6 oz/ 315 yds/170g per skein):
  - 3 oz/150 yds/85g #9607 limelight
  - ¼ oz/13 yds/7g #9601 coconut
- Black embroidery floss
- Sizes F/5/3.75mm and H/8/5mm crochet hooks or sizes needed to obtain gauge
- Tapestry needle
- Fiberfill
- Stitch marker

GAUGE
Size F hook: 5 sc = 1 inch; 5 sc rows = 1 inch

Size H hook: Rnds 1–3 of Blanket = 3 inches square

PATTERN NOTES
Join with slip stitch as indicated unless otherwise stated.

Chain-3 at beginning of row or round counts as first double crochet unless otherwise stated.

Work in continuous rounds, do not turn or join unless otherwise stated.

Mark first stitch of each round.

SPECIAL STITCH
Picot: Ch 2, sl st in 2nd ch from hook.

INSTRUCTIONS
BLANKET
Rnd 1: With limelight and size H hook, ch 4, sl st in first ch to form ring, **ch 3** *(see Pattern Notes)*, 11 dc in ring, **join** *(see Pattern Notes)* in 3rd ch of beg ch-3. *(12 dc)*

Rnd 2: Ch 3, *(2 dc, tr) in next st, (tr, 2 dc) in next st**, dc in next st, rep from * around, ending last rep at **, join in 3rd ch of beg ch-3. *(8 tr, 20 dc)*

Rnd 3: Ch 3, dc in each of next 2 dc, *(2 dc, tr) in next tr, (tr, 2 dc) in next tr**, dc in each of next 5 sts, rep from * around, ending last rep at **, dc in each of last 2 sts, join in 3rd ch of beg ch-3. *(8 tr, 36 dc)*

Rnd 4: Ch 3, dc in each of next 4 sts, *(2 dc, tr) in next tr, (tr, 2 dc) in next tr**, dc in each of next 9 sts, rep from * around, ending last rep at **, dc in each of last 4 sts, join in 3rd ch of beg ch-3. *(8 tr, 52 dc)*

Rnd 5: Ch 3, dc in each of next 6 sts, *(2 dc, tr) in next tr, (tr, 2 dc) in next tr**, dc in each of next 13 sts, rep from * around, ending last rep at **, dc in each of last 6 sts, join in 3rd ch of beg ch-3. *(8 tr, 68 dc)*

Rnd 6: Ch 3, dc in each of next 8 sts, *(2 dc, tr) in next tr, (tr, 2 dc) in next tr**, dc in each of next 17 sts, rep from * around, ending last rep at **, dc in each of last 8 sts, join in 3rd ch of beg ch-3. *(8 tr, 84 dc)*

Rnd 7: Ch 3, dc in each of next 10 sts, *(2 dc, tr) in next tr, (tr, 2 dc) in next tr**, dc in each of next 21 sts, rep from * around, ending last rep at **, dc in each of last 10 sts, join in 3rd ch of beg ch-3. *(8 tr, 100 dc)*

Rnd 8: Ch 3, dc in each of next 12 sts, *(2 dc, tr) in next tr, (tr, 2 dc) in next tr**, dc in each of next 25 sts, rep from * around, ending last rep at **, dc in each of last 12 sts, join in 3rd ch of beg ch-3. *(8 tr, 116 dc)*

Rnd 9: Ch 3, dc in each of next 14 sts, *(2 dc, tr) in next tr, (tr, 2 dc) in next tr**, dc in each of next 29 sts, rep from * around, ending last rep at **, dc in each of last 14 sts, join in 3rd ch of beg ch-3. *(8 tr, 132 dc)*

Rnd 10: Ch 3, dc in each of next 16 sts, *(2 dc, tr) in next tr, (tr, 2 dc) in next tr**, dc in each of next 33 sts, rep from * around, ending last rep at **, dc in each of last 16 sts, join in 3rd ch of beg ch-3. *(8 tr, 148 dc)*

TRIM

Rnd 11: Working in **back lps** *(see Stitch Guide)*, ch 1, sc in each sc around with 2 sc in each tr at each corner, join in beg sc.

Rnd 12: Working in back lps, ch 1, sc in each of first 2 sts, ***picot** *(see Special Stitch)***, sc in each of next 2 sts, rep from * around, ending last rep at **, join in beg sc. Fasten off.

HEAD

Rnd 1: With size F hook and limelight, make **slip ring** *(see Fig. 1)*, 6 sc in ring, pull to close ring, **do not join** *(see Pattern Notes)*. *(6 sc)*

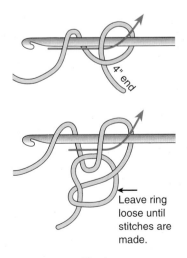

4" end

Leave ring loose until stitches are made.

Fig. 1
Slip Ring

Rnd 2: 2 sc in each st around. *(12 sc)*

Rnd 3: [2 sc in next st, sc in next st] around. *(18 sc)*

Rnd 4: [2 sc in next st, sc in each of next 2 sts] around. *(24 sc)*

Rnd 5: [2 sc in next st, sc in each of next 3 sts] around. *(30 sc)*

Rnds 6–10: Sc in each st around.

Rnd 11: [**Sc dec** *(see Stitch Guide)* in next 2 sts, sc in each of next 3 sts] around. *(24 sc)*

Rnd 12: [Sc dec in next 2 sts, sc in each of next 2 sts] around. Stuff Head. *(18 sc)*

Rnd 13: [Sc dec in next 2 sts, sc in next st] around. Finish stuffing Head. *(12 sc)*

Rnd 14: [Sc dec in next 2 sts] around. *(6 sc)*

FIRST ARM
Rnd 15: 2 sc in each of next 3 sts, leaving rem sts unworked, turn. *(6 sc)*

Rnds 16 & 17: Sc in each st around.

Rnd 18: 2 sc in each st around. *(12 sc)*

Rnds 19–26: Sc in each st around. Lightly stuff Arm.

Row 27: Flatten last rnd, working through both thicknesses, [ch 3, sc in next st] across, turn.

Row 28: (Sl st, dc, sl st) in each ch sp across. Fasten off.

2ND ARM
Rnd 15: Join limelight with sc in first unworked st on rnd 14 of Head, sc in same st, 2 sc in each of next 2 sts, turn. *(6 sc)*

Rnds 16 & 17: Sc in each st around.

Rnd 18: 2 sc in each st around. *(12 sc)*

Rnds 19–26: Sc in each st around. Lightly stuff Arm.

Row 27: Flatten last rnd, working through both thicknesses, [ch 3, sc in next st] across, turn.

Row 28: (Sl st, dc, sl st) in each ch sp across. Fasten off.

EYE
MAKE 2.
Rnd 1: With size F hook and coconut, make slip ring, 5 sc in ring, pull to close ring. *(5 sc)*

Rnd 2: 2 sc in first st, [sc in next st, 2 sc in next st] twice, **changing colors** *(see Stitch Guide)* to limelight in last st. *(8 sc)*

Rnd 3: Working in **front lps** *(see Stitch Guide)*, sl st in each st around, join in beg sl st.

Rnd 4: Working in back lps of rnd 2, ch 1, 2 sc in first st, sc in next st, [2 sc in next st, sc in next st] around, **do not join**. *(12 sc)*

Rnd 5: Sc in each st around.

Rnd 6: [Sc dec in next 2 sts] around. Leaving long end, fasten off.

Stuff.

Weave long end through top of sts on last rnd, pull to close. Secure end.

FINISHING
Using **straight stitch** *(see Fig. 2)*, with black embroidery floss, make 1 straight stitch in each Eye as shown in photo.

Fig. 2
Straight Stitch

Using straight stitch, with black floss, embroider mouth in smile as shown in photo.

Sew Head to center of Blanket, making sure Arms are extended on either side of Head. ■

Little Man Ensemble

DESIGN BY **SUE CHILDRESS**

FINISHED SIZES

Instructions given fit 24 months (*small*); changes for size 2 toddler (*medium*) are in [ ].

FINISHED GARMENT MEASUREMENTS

Chest: 20 inches (*small*) [22 inches (*medium*)]

MATERIALS

- Katia Cotton Comfort light (DK) weight yarn (1¾ oz/180 yds/50g per ball):
  - 4 [5] balls #7 blue
  - 2 [2] balls #1 white
- Size F/5/3.75mm crochet hook or size needed to obtain gauge
- Tapestry needle
- Sewing needle
- Blue sewing thread
- ½ inch buttons: 5 [6]

GAUGE

6 hdc = 1 inch; 9 hdc rows = 2½ inches

PATTERN NOTES

Chain-2 at beginning of row or round does not count as first half double crochet unless otherwise stated.

Chain-3 at beginning of row or round counts as first double crochet unless otherwise stated.

Join with slip stitch as indicated unless otherwise stated.

INSTRUCTIONS
SWEATER
BODY
FIRST FRONT

Row 1: With blue, ch 36 [46], hdc in 3rd ch from hook (*first 2 chs count as first hdc*) and in each ch across, turn. (*35 [45] hdc*)

Row 2: Working in **back lps** (*see Stitch Guide*) of this and each rem row, **ch 2** (*see Pattern Notes*), hdc in first st and in each st across to last 2 sts, 2 hdc in each of last 2 sts, turn. (*37 [47] hdc*)

Row 3: **Ch 3** (*see Pattern Notes*), dc in same st, 2 dc in next st, hdc in each of last 35 [45] sts, turn. (*39 [49] sts*)

Row 4: Ch 2, hdc in first st and in each st across to last 2 sts, 2 dc in each of last 2 sts, turn. (*41 [51] sts*)

Row 5: Ch 3, dc in same st, 2 dc in next st, hdc in each st across, turn. (*43 [53] sts*)

Row 6: Ch 2, hdc in first st and in each st across to last 2 sts, 2 dc in each of last 2 sts, turn. (*45 [55] sts*)

Row 7: Ch 3, dc in same st, 2 dc in next st, hdc in each st across, turn. *(47 [57] sts)*

Row 8: Ch 2, hdc in first st and in each st across to last 2 sts, 2 dc in each of last 2 sts, turn. *(49 [59] sts)*

Rows 9–15 [9–17]: Ch 2, hdc in first st and in each st across, turn.

FIRST ARMHOLE SHAPING

Row 16 [18]: Ch 2, hdc in first st and in each of next 28 [38] sts, leaving rem sts unworked, turn. *(29 [39] hdc)*

Row 17 [19]: Ch 2, hdc in first st and in each st across, turn.

Row 18 [20]: Ch 2, hdc in first st and each st across, ch 21, turn.

BACK
FIRST SHOULDER

Row 19 [21]: Hdc in 3rd ch from hook (*first 2 chs count as first hdc*), hdc in each ch and in each st across, turn. *(49 [59] hdc)*

Rows 20–25 [22–29]: Ch 2, hdc in first st and in each st across, turn.

NECK SHAPING

Row 26 [30]: Ch 2, hdc in first st and in each st across, leaving last 2 sts unworked, turn. *(47 [57] hdc)*

Row 27 [31]: Sl st in each of first 3 sts, ch 2, hdc in same st and in each st across, turn. *(45 [55] hdc)*

Row 28 [32]: Rep row 26 [30]. *(43 [53] hdc)*

Rows 29–41 [33–45]: Ch 2, hdc in first st and in each st across, turn.

Row 42 [46]: Ch 2, hdc in first st and in each st across, turn.

Row 43 [47]: Ch 3, hdc in 2nd ch from hook, hdc in each ch and in each st across, turn. *(45 [55] hdc)*

Row 44 [48]: Ch 2, hdc in first st and in each st across with 3 hdc in last st, turn. *(47 [57] hdc)*

Row 45 [49]: Rep row 43 [47]. *(49 [59] hdc)*

2ND SHOULDER

Rows 46–51 [50–57]: Ch 2, hdc in first st and in each st across, turn.

2ND ARMHOLE SHAPING

Row 52 [58]: Ch 2, hdc in first st and in each of next 28 [38] sts, leaving rem sts unworked, turn. *(29 [39] hdc)*

Row 53 [59]: Ch 2, hdc in first st and in each st across, turn.

Row 54 [60]: Ch 2, hdc in first st and each st across, ch 21, turn.

2ND FRONT

Row 55 [61]: Hdc in 3rd ch from hook (*first 2 chs count as first hdc*), hdc in each ch and in each st across, turn. *(49 [59] hdc)*

Rows 56–60 [62–68]: Ch 2, hdc in first st and in each st across, turn.

Row 61 [69]: Ch 2, hdc in first st and in each st across, leaving last 2 sts unworked, turn. *(47 [57] hdc)*

Row 62 [70]: Ch 2, sk first st, **hdc dec** (*see Stitch Guide*) in first 2 sts, hdc in each st across, turn. *(45 [55] hdc)*

Row 63 [71]: Ch 2, hdc in first st and in each st across, leaving last 2 sts unworked, turn. *(43 [53] hdc)*

Row 64 [72]: Ch 2, sk first st, hdc dec in next 2 sts, hdc in each st across, turn. *(41 [51] hdc)*

Row 65 [73]: Ch 2, hdc in first st and in each st across, leaving last 2 sts unworked, turn. *(39 [49] hdc)*

Row 66 [74]: Ch 2, hdc dec in next 2 sts, hdc in each st across, turn. *(38 [48] hdc)*

Row 67 [75]: Ch 2, hdc in first st and in each st across, leaving last 2 sts unworked, turn. *(36 [46] hdc)*

Row 68 [76]: Ch 2, hdc dec in next 2 sts, hdc in each st across, turn. *(35 [45] hdc)*

Row 69 [77]: Ch 2, hdc in first st and in each st across, **do not turn.**

Sew shoulder seams.

EDGING
Rnd 1: Working in ends of rows and in sts, ch 1, evenly sp sc around, **join** *(see Pattern Notes)* in beg sc. Fasten off.

Rnd 2: Join white with sc in first st, sc in each st around to first shoulder seam working 2 sc in corners, 2 sc in seam, [sc in each of next 3 sts, **sc dec** *(see Stitch Guide)* in next 2 sts] across to next shoulder seam, 2 sc in seam, sc in each rem st around with 2 sc in each corner, join in beg sc.

Rnd 3: Ch 1, sc in each st around with 2 sc in each corner, join in beg sc.

Rnd 4: Ch 1, sc in each st across to first shoulder seam with 2 sc in corner, [sc in each of next 3 sts, sc dec in next 2 sts] across to next shoulder seam, sc in each rem st around with 2 sc in each corner, join in beg sc.

Rnd 5: Ch 1, sc in each st across right side with 2 sc in corner, sc around neck edge, 2 sc in corner, ch 2, sk next 2 sc *(buttonhole)*, [sc in each of next 6 sts, ch 2, sk next 2 sts] 4 [5] times across left side *(reverse for girls with buttonholes on right side)*, 2 sc at corner, sc in each rem st around, join in beg sc.

Rnd 6: Ch 1, sc in each st around with 2 sc in each corner and in each ch sp, join in beg sc.

Rnd 7: Ch 1, sc in each st around with 2 sc in each corner, join in beg sc. Fasten off.

SLEEVE
Rnd 1: Working around 1 armhole, in ends of rows and in sts, join blue in center bottom of armhole, **ch 2** *(now counts as first hdc)*, hdc in same row, evenly sp 44 [54] hdc around, join in 2nd ch of beg ch-2. *(46 [56] sts)*

Rnd 2: Work all rem rnds in back lps, ch 2, hdc in each of next 13 [19] sts, dc dec in next 2 sts, dc

in each of next 16 [18] sts, dc dec in next 2 sts, hdc in each rem st around, join in 2nd ch of beg ch-2. *(44 [54] sts)*

Rnd 3: Ch 2, hdc in each of next 12 [16] sts, dc dec in next 2 sts, dc in each of next 14 [16] sts, dc dec in next 2 sts, hdc in each rem st around, join in 2nd ch of beg ch-2. *(42 [52] sts)*

Rnds 4–15 [4–18]: Ch 2, hdc in each of next 12 [16] sts, dc in each of next 14 [16] sts, hdc in each rem st around, join in 2nd ch of beg ch-2.

Rnds 16 & 17 [19 & 20]: Ch 2, hdc in each st around, join in 2nd ch of beg ch-2.

Rnd 18 [21]: Working in both lps, ch 1, sk first st, sc in next st, [sc dec in next 2 sts, sc in each of next 3 sts] around, join in beg sc. Fasten off.

CUFF
Rnd 1: Join white with sc in first st, sc in each st around, **do not join.**

Rnds 2–6: Sc in each st around. At end of last rnd, join in beg sc. Fasten off.

Sew buttons to other front opposite buttonhole.

CAP
Rnd 1: With blue, ch 3, 8 hdc in 3rd ch from hook, join in top of beg ch-3, sl st in next st. *(9 hdc)*

Rnd 2: Working rem rnds in back lps, ch 2, hdc in same st, 2 hdc in each st around, join in 2nd ch of beg ch-2, sl st in next st, **turn.** *(18 hdc)*

Rnd 3: Ch 2, 2 hdc in next st, [hdc in next st, 2 hdc in next st] around, join in 2nd ch of beg ch-2, turn. *(27 hdc)*

Rnds 4–6: Ch 2, hdc in same st, hdc in each of next 2 sts, [2 hdc in next st, hdc in each of next 2 sts] around, join in 2nd ch of beg ch-2, turn. *(64 hdc at end of last rnd)*

Rnds 7 & 8: Ch 2, hdc in each of next 2 sts, 2 hdc in next st, [hdc in each of next 3 sts, 2 hdc in next st] around, join in 2nd ch of beg ch-2, turn. *(100 hdc at end of last rnd)*

Rnd 9: Ch 2, hdc in each of next 3 sts, [hdc in each of next 4 sts, 2 hdc in next st] around, join in 2nd ch of beg ch-2, turn. *(120 hdc)*

Rnds 10–15: Ch 2, hdc in each st around, join in 2nd ch of beg ch-2.

Rnd 16: Working in both lps, ch 1, sc in each of first 3 sts, [sc dec in next 2 sts, sc in each of next 3 sts] around, ending with sc dec in last 2 sts, join in beg sc. Fasten off. *(96 sc)*

Rnd 17: Join white with sc in first st, sc in next st, sc dec in next 2 sts, [sc in each of next 2 sts, sc dec in next 2 sts] around, **do not join**.

Rnds 18–22: Sc in each st around. At end of last rnd, join in beg sc. Fasten off.

BOOTIE
MAKE 2.

Rnd 1: With blue, ch 10, 2 hdc in 3rd ch from hook, sc in each of next 6 chs, 5 dc in last ch, working on opposite side of ch, sc in each of next 6 chs, hdc in last ch, join in 2nd ch of beg ch-2. *(21 sts)*

Rnd 2: Ch 2, hdc in same st, 2 hdc in each of next 2 sts, hdc in each of next 6 sts, [2 hdc in next st, hdc in next st] twice, 2 hdc in next st, hdc in each of next 6 sts, 2 hdc in last st, join in 2nd ch of beg ch-2. *(28 hdc)*

Rnd 3: Ch 2, hdc in same st, 2 hdc in each of next 3 sts, sc in each of next 8 sts, hdc in next st, 2 dc in each of next 5 sts, hdc in next st, sc in each of next 9 sts, join in 2nd ch of beg ch-2. *(37 sts)*

Rnd 4: Ch 1, sc in each of first 19 sts, hdc in next st, 2 hdc in each of next 4 sts, hdc in next st, sc in each of last 12 sts, join in beg sc. *(41 sts)*

Rnd 5: Working rem rnds in back lps, ch 2, hdc in each st around, join in 2nd ch of beg ch-2, **turn.**

Rnds 6 & 7: Ch 2, hdc in each st around, join in 2nd ch of beg ch-2, turn.

Rnd 8: Ch 2, hdc in each of next 9 sts, [dc dec in next 3 sts] 5 times, hdc in each rem st around, join in 2nd ch of beg ch-2, turn. *(31 sts)*

Rnd 9: Ch 1, sc in each of first 16 sts, [dc dec in next 3 sts] twice, sc in each rem st around, join in beg sc, turn. *(27 sts)*

Rnd 10: Working in both lps, ch 1, sc in each st around, join in beg sc. Fasten off.

Rnd 11: Join white in center back st, working from left to right, **reverse sc** *(see Fig. 1)* around, join in beg reverse sc. Fasten off.

TRIM
Working in rem lps on rnd 4, join blue with sc at center back, sc in each lp around, join in beg sc. Fasten off.

TIE
With blue, ch 50. Fasten off.

Weave Tie through sts on rnd 10, beg and end in front.

Tie ends in bow. ∎

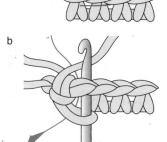
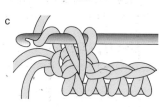

Fig. 1
Reverse Single Crochet

Short Top
Baby Socks

DESIGN BY **DIANE SIMPSON**

SKILL LEVEL

EASY

FINISHED SIZES

Instructions given fit newborn–3 months; changes for 3–6 months, 6–9 months and 9–12 months are in [ ].

MATERIALS

- Red Heart LusterSheen fine (sport) weight yarn (4 oz/335 yds/113g per skein):
  Solid Socks:
  1 [1¼, 1½, 1¾] oz/100 [125, 150, 175] yds/28 [35, 43, 50]g #0001 white or #0615 tea leaf
  Two-Color Socks:
  ½ [¾, ¾, 1] oz/ 50 [75, 75, 100] yds/14 [21, 21 28]g each #0001 white and #0615 tea leaf
- Size hook needed for size listed in gauge or size needed to obtain gauge
- Stitch marker

GAUGE

Size F/5/3.75mm crochet hook *(newborn–3 months)*: Rnds 1–3 = 1 inch

Size G/6/4mm crochet hook *(3–6 months)*: Rnds 1–3 = 1¼ inches

Size H/8/5mm crochet hook *(6–9 months)*: Rnds 1–3 = 1½ inches

Size I/9/5.5mm crochet hook *(9–12 months)*: Rnds 1–3 = 1¾ inches

PATTERN NOTES

Work in continuous rounds, do not turn or join unless otherwise stated.

Mark first stitch of each round.

Work all rows in **back loops** *(see Stitch Guide)* unless otherwise stated.

Join with slip stitch as indicated unless otherwise stated.

INSTRUCTIONS
SOLID SOCK
MAKE 2.
TOE

Rnd 1 (RS): Make **slip ring** (*see Fig. 1*), ch 1, 6 sc in ring, tighten ring, **do not join** (*see Pattern Notes*). (*6 sc*)

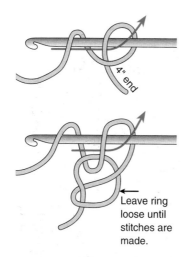

Fig. 1
Slip Ring

Rnd 2: 2 sc in each st around. (*12 sc*)

Rnd 3: [2 sc in next st, sc in next st] around. (*18 sc*)

TOP

Row 4: Now working in rows, ch 18, sc in 2nd ch from hook and in each ch across, sl st in each of next 2 sts on Toe, turn. (*17 sc*)

Row 5: Sk sl sts, sc in each sc across, turn.

Row 6: Ch 1, sc in each sc across, sl st in each of next 2 sts on Toe, turn.

Rows 7 & 8: Rep rows 5 and 6.

Row 9: Sk sl sts, sc in each of first 8 sts, leaving rem sts unworked, turn. (*8 sc*)

Rows 10–15: [Rep rows 6 and 5 alternately] 3 times.

Row 16: Ch 10, sc in 2nd ch from hook, sc in each ch across, sl st in each of next 2 sts on Toe, turn.

Rows 17–20: [Rep rows 5 and 6 alternately] 4 times, turn.

Row 21: Sk sl sts, sc in each sc across, turn.

Row 22: Turn WS out, working through both thicknesses, sl st rows 4 and 21 tog. Fasten off.

Flatten Sock creating an L shape, sew ends of rows tog to form heel.

CUFF

Rnd 1: Join with sl st in first st to left of heel seam, ch 1, sc in each st across row 8, sc in end of each of next 7 rows, sc in ch on opposite side of row 16, **join** (*see Pattern Notes*) in beg sc. (*25 sc*)

Row 2: Now working in rows, ch 7, sc in 2nd ch from hook and in each ch across, sl st in each of next 2 sts on rnd 1, turn.

Row 3: Sk sl sts, sc in each sc across, turn.

Row 4: Ch 1, sc in each sc across, sl st in each of next 2 sts on rnd 1, turn.

Rows 5–24: [Rep rows 3 and 4 alternately] 10 times.

Row 25: Turn WS out, working through both thicknesses, sl st row 24 and starting ch on opposite side of ch-7 on row 2 tog. Fasten off.

TWO-COLOR SOCK
MAKE 2.
TOE

Rnds 1–3: With first color, work same as rnds 1–3 on Toe of Solid Sock. At end of last rnd, fasten off.

TOP

Row 4: Now working in rows, join 2nd color with sl st in first sc, ch 18, sc in 2nd ch from hook and in each ch across, sl st in each of next 2 sts on Toe, turn. (*17 sc*)

Rows 5–22: Work same as rows 5–22 of Top on Solid Sock.

CUFF

With first color, work Cuff of Solid Sock. ■

love stitches
for Charities

Go Red
Heart
Pillow
DESIGN BY **DONNA SCOTT**

SKILL LEVEL

EASY

FINISHED SIZE
15½ x 16 inches

MATERIALS
- Red Heart Super Saver medium (worsted) weight yarn (7 oz/364 yds/198g per skein):
    1 skein #390 hot red
- Size H/8/5mm crochet hook or size needed to obtain gauge
- Tapestry needle
- Sewing needle
- Red sewing thread
- Red fabric: ½ yd
- Fiberfill

GAUGE
3 sc = 1 inch; 10 sc rows = 3 inch

PATTERN NOTE
Join with slip stitch as indicated unless otherwise stated.

INSTRUCTIONS
PILLOW
HEART SIDE
MAKE 2.

Row 1: Beg at point, ch 2, sc in 2nd ch from hook, turn. *(1 sc)*

Row 2: Ch 1, 3 sc in st, turn. *(3 sc)*

Row 3: Ch 1, 2 sc in first st, sc in next st, 2 sc in last st, turn. *(5 sc)*

Row 4: Ch 1, 2 sc in first st, sc in each st across with 2 sc in last st, turn. *(7 sc)*

Row 5: Ch 1, sc in each st across, turn.

Rows 6–8: Ch 1, 2 sc in first st, sc in each st across with 2 sc in last st, turn. *(13 sc at end of last row)*

Row 9: Ch 1, sc in each st across, turn.

Rows 10–12: Ch 1, 2 sc in first st, sc in each st across with 2 sc in last st, turn. *(19 sc at end of last row)*

Row 13: Ch 1, sc in each st across, turn.

Rows 14–16: Ch 1, 2 sc in first st, sc in each st across with 2 sc in last st, turn. *(25 sc at end of last row)*

Row 17: Ch 1, sc in each st across, turn.

Rows 18–20: Ch 1, 2 sc in first st, sc in each st across with 2 sc in last st, turn. *(31 sc at end of last row)*

Row 21: Ch 1, sc in each st across, turn.

Rows 22–24: Ch 1, 2 sc in first st, sc in each st across with 2 sc in last st, turn. *(37 sc at end of last row)*

Row 25: Ch 1, sc in each st across, turn.

Rows 26–28: Ch 1, 2 sc in first st, sc in each st across with 2 sc in last st, turn. *(43 sc at end of last row)*

Rows 29–38: Ch 1, sc in each st across, turn.

FIRST LOBE

Row 1: Ch 1, sc in each of first 22 sts, leaving rem sts unworked, turn. *(22 sc)*

Rows 2–7: Ch 1, sk first st, sc in each st across, turn. *(16 sc at end of last row)*

Rows 8–12: Ch 1, sk first st, sc in each st across, ending with **sc dec** *(see Stitch Guide)* in last 2 sts, turn. At end of last row, fasten off. *(6 sc at end of last row)*

2ND LOBE

Row 1: With First Lobe to the right, join with sc in same st at center as last sc of row 1 on First Lobe, sc in each of next 21 sts, turn. *(22 sc)*

Rows 2–7: Ch 1, sk first st, sc in each st across, turn. *(16 sc at end of last row)*

Rows 8–12: Ch 1, sk first st, sc in each st across, ending with sc dec in last 2 sts, turn. At end of last row, fasten off. *(6 sc at end of last row)*

PILLOW FORM

Using 1 Heart Side as pattern, cut 2 pieces from fabric ¼ inch larger around all edges.

With RS tog, allowing ¼ inch seam, sew fabric pieces tog, leaving 4 inches unsewn.

Turn RS out. Stuff.

Sew opening closed.

EDGING

Rnd 1: Holding Heart Sides tog, working through both thicknesses in ends of rows and in sts, join with sc in starting ch on opposite side of row 1, 2 sc in same ch, evenly sp 136 sc around, inserting Pillow Form before closing, **join** *(see Pattern Note)* in beg sc.

Rnd 2: Working in **back lps** *(see Stitch Guide)*, ch 1, sc in first st, ch 3, [sc in next st, ch 3] around, join in beg sc. Fasten off. ∎

Go Red
Purse

DESIGN BY **SANDY SCOVILLE**

SKILL LEVEL

INTERMEDIATE

FINISHED SIZE
9 inches diameter x 14½ inches high

MATERIALS
- Omega Nylon Cord #18 (7 oz/ 197 yds per spool): 4 spools red
- Size G/6/4mm crochet hook or size needed to obtain gauge
- Tapestry needle
- Stitch marker

GAUGE
Base: Rnds 1 & 2 = 2 inches in diameter

Body: 4 pattern rows = 2 inches

PATTERN NOTES
Work in continuous rounds; do not turn or join unless otherwise stated.

Mark first stitch of each round.

SPECIAL STITCHES
V-stitch (V-st): (Dc, ch 1, dc) in place indicated.

Shell: 5 dc in place indicated.

INSTRUCTIONS

PURSE

BASE

Rnd 1: Ch 4, sl st in first ch to form ring, ch 1, 8 sc in ring, **do not join** (see Pattern Notes). (8 sc)

Rnd 2: 2 sc in each st around. (16 sc)

Rnd 3: [2 sc in next sc, sc in next sc] around. (24 sc)

Rnd 4: [2 sc in next st, sc in each of next 2 sts] around. (32 sc)

Rnd 5: [2 sc in next st, sc in each of next 3 sts] around. (40 sc)

Rnd 6: [2 sc in next st, sc in each of next 4 sts] around. (48 sc)

Rnd 7: [2 sc in next st, sc in each of next 5 sts] around. (56 sc)

Rnd 8: [2 sc in next st, sc in each of next 6 sts] around. (64 sc)

Rnd 9: [2 sc in next st, sc in each of next 7 sts] around. (72 sc)

Rnd 10: [2 sc in next st, sc in each of next 8 sts] around. (80 sc)

Rnd 11: [2 sc in next st, sc in each of next 9 sts] around. (88 sc)

Rnd 12: [2 sc in next st, sc in each of next 10 sts] around. (96 sc)

Rnd 13: [2 sc in next st, sc in each of next 11 sts] around. (104 sc)

Rnd 14: [2 sc in next st, sc in each of next 12 sts] around. (112 sc)

Rnd 15: [2 sc in next st, sc in each of next 13 sts] around. (120 sc)

BODY

Rnd 1: [Sk next 2 sc, **V-st** (see Special Stitches) in next sc, sk next 2 sc, sc in next sc] around, **do not join.**

Rnd 2: [**Shell** (see Special Stitches) in ch sp of next V-st, sc in next sc] around. (20 shells)

Rnd 3: Sc in each of next 3 dc, V-st in next sc, [sk next 2 dc, sc in next dc, V-st in next sc] around.

Rnd 4: Sk next 2 sc, *sc in next sc, shell in ch sp of next V-st, rep from * 19 times.

Rnd 5: [V-st in next sc, sk next 2 dc, sc in next dc, sk next 2 dc] around.

Rnds 6–21: [Rep rnds 2–5 consecutively] 4 times.

Rnd 22: [Shell in ch sp of next V-st, sc in next sc] around.

Rnd 23: Sc in each of next 3 dc, ch 2, sk next 2 dc, V-st in next sc, ch 2, [sk next 2 dc, sc in next dc, ch 2, sk next 2 dc, V-st in next sc, ch 2] 19 times, sk next 2 sc at beg of rnd, hdc in next sc.

TOP BAND

Rnd 24: 3 hdc in next ch-2 sp, 2 hdc in next ch-1 sp, [2 hdc in each of next 2 ch-2 sps, hdc in next ch-1 sp] 9 times, 3 hdc in each of next 2 ch-2 sps, hdc in next ch-1 sp, [2 hdc in each of next 2 ch-2 sps, hdc in next ch-1 sp] 9 times, 2 hdc in next ch-2 sp. (104 hdc)

Rnd 25: [Ch 2, sk next 2 hdc, hdc in each of next 11 hdc] around. (8 ch-2 sps)

Rnd 26: [2 hdc in next ch-2 sp, hdc in each of next 11 hdc] around. (104 hdc)

Rnds 27 & 28: Hdc in each hdc around.

Rnd 29: Hdc in each hdc around, join with sc in first hdc. Fasten off.

SLIDE FOR STRAPS

Row 1: Ch 5, sc in 2nd ch from hook and in each ch across, turn. (4 sc)

Row 2: Sc in each sc across, turn.

Rows 3–14: Rep row 2.

Fold piece with WS tog, working in opposite side of starting ch and in last sc row, sl st in each of next 4 sts. Leaving 12-inch end, fasten off.

PATCH COVER

Row 1: Ch 7, sc in 2nd ch from hook and in each of next 5 chs, turn. *(6 sc)*

Row 2: Ch 1, sc in each sc across, turn.

Rows 3–6: Rep row 2. At end of last row, fasten off.

EDGING

Working along side edge, sc in end of each row, working on opposite side of starting ch, 2 sc in next ch, sc in each of next 4 chs, 2 sc in next ch, working along next side edge, sc in end of each row across, working in sts along next side edge, 2 sc in first st, sc in each of next 4 sts, 2 sc in last st, join in beg sc. Leaving long end, fasten off.

STRAP

Ch 301, sc in 2nd ch from hook and in each ch across. Leaving long end, fasten off.

FINISHING

1. Weave Strap in and out of ch-2 sps on rnd 25, beg on right side in sp to right of joining of rnd 29 and ending in sp to left of joining.

2. Flatten Slide, with long end, sew across center, forming 2 holes.

3. Push Strap ends through Slide holes, slip Slide upward to pull Purse closed.

4. Being careful not to twist Strap, place ends side by side near Base of Purse directly beneath Slide. With RS of Patch facing, cover Strap ends as shown in Assembly Diagram. Sew Patch in place, catching Strap ends. ∎

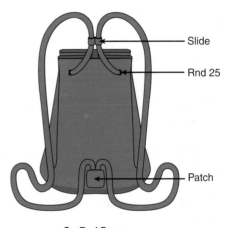

Go Red Purse
Diagram

Sonoma Shawl

DESIGN BY **DARLA SIMS**

SKILL LEVEL

EASY

FINISHED SIZE
15 x 72 inches

MATERIALS
- Red Heart Soft Yarn medium (worsted) weight yarn (5 oz/256 yds/140g per skein):
    3 skeins #5142 cherry red
- Size I/9/5.5mm crochet hook or size needed to obtain gauge

GAUGE
2 pattern reps = 6 inches

PATTERN NOTE
Chain-3 at beginning of row or round counts as first double crochet unless otherwise stated.

INSTRUCTIONS
SHAWL

Row 1: Ch 51, dc in 4th ch from hook (*first 3 chs count as first dc*), *sk next 2 chs, 5 dc in next ch, sk next 2 chs**, dc in each of next 5 chs, rep from * across, ending last rep at **, dc in each of last 2 chs, turn.

Row 2: Ch 3 (*see Pattern Note*), dc in next st, *sk next 2 sts, 5 dc in next st, sk next 2 sts**, dc in each of next 5 sts, rep from * across, ending last rep at **, dc in each of last 2 sts, turn.

Next rows: Rep row 2 until piece measures 70½ inches from beg. At end of last row, **do not turn or fasten off.**

EDGING

Working around outer edge in sts, in ends of rows and in starting ch on opposite side of row 1, ch 1, evenly sp sc across, working in starting ch opposite side of row 1, 3 sc in first ch, sc in next ch, sk next 2 chs, [5 dc in next ch, sk next 4 chs] 8 times, 5 dc in next ch, sk next 2 chs, sc in next ch, 3 sc in last ch, evenly sp sc in ends of rows across, 3 sc in first st, sc in next st, sk next 2 sts, 5 dc in next st, [sk next 4 sts, 5 dc in next st] across to last 4 sts, sk next 2 sts, sc in next st, 3 sc in last st, join with sl st in beg sc. Fasten off. ■

Chemo Hats

DESIGN BY **KIM KOTARY**

SKILL LEVEL

INTERMEDIATE

FINISHED SIZE
Adult: 1 size fits most

MATERIALS
- Red Heart Eco-Cotton Blend medium (worsted) weight cotton yarn (3 oz/145 yds/85g per ball): 1 ball each #1645 moss *(Hat #1)*, #1370 candy marl *(Hat #2)* and #1340 almond *(Hat #3)*
- Sizes H/8/5mm and J/10/6mm crochet hooks or size needed to obtain gauge
- Tapestry needle

4 MEDIUM

GAUGE
Size J hook: 13 sc = 4 inches; 15 sc rnds = 4 inches

PATTERN NOTES
Use size J hook unless otherwise stated.

Work in continuous rounds, do not join or turn unless otherwise stated.

Mark first stitch of each round.

Join with slip stitch as indicated unless otherwise stated.

INSTRUCTIONS
HAT #1
Rnd 1: With moss and **size J hook** *(see Pattern Notes)*, ch 2, 6 sc in 2nd ch from hook, **do not join** *(see Pattern Notes)*. *(6 sc)*

Rnd 2: 2 sc in each sc around. *(12 sc)*

Rnd 3: [2 sc in next sc, tr in next sc] around. *(18 sts)*

Rnd 4: [2 sc in next sc, sc in each st around to next tr, tr in next tr] around.

Next rnds: Rep last rnd until there are 66 sts.

Next rnds: Work even until piece measures 8 inches from beg. At end of last rnd, **join** *(see Pattern Notes)* in beg sc.

Last rnd: Ch 1, working from left to right, **reverse sc** *(see Fig. 1)* in each st around, join in beg reverse sc. Fasten off.

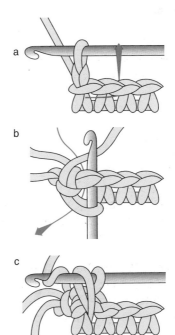

Fig. 1
Reverse Single Crochet

HAT #2

Rnd 1: With candy marl and **size J hook** (*see Pattern Notes*), ch 2, 6 sc in 2nd ch from hook, **do not join** (*see Pattern Notes*). (*6 sc*)

Rnd 2: 2 sc in each sc around. (*12 sc*)

Rnd 3: [2 sc in next sc, tr in next sc] around. (*18 sts*)

Rnd 4: [2 sc in next sc, sc in each st around to next tr, tr in next tr] around.

Next rnds: Rep last rnd until there are 66 sts.

Next rnds: Work even until piece measures 8 inches from beg. At end of last rnd, **join** (*see Pattern Notes*) in beg sc.

Last rnd: Ch 1, sc in first st, *sk next st, 5 dc in next st, sk next st**, sc in next st, rep from * around, ending last rep at **, join in beg sc. Fasten off.

FLOWER

Rnd 1: With candy marl, ch 5, sl st in first ch to form ring, [ch 3, sl st in ring] 6 times, **do not join.** (*6 ch sps*)

Rnd 2: Ch 1, (sc, hdc, 3 dc, hdc, sc) in each ch sp around. (*6 petals*)

Rnd 3: Working behind last rnd, sl st in center ring, [ch 5, sl st in center ring] 6 times. (*6 ch sps*)

Rnd 4: (Sc, hdc, dc, 3 tr, dc, hdc, sc) in each ch sp around. Fasten off. (*6 petals*)

Sew Flower to Hat.

HAT #3

Rnd 1: With almond and **size J hook** (*see Pattern Notes*), ch 2, 6 sc in 2nd ch from hook, **do not join** (*see Pattern Notes*). (*6 sc*)

Rnd 2: 2 sc in each sc around. (*12 sc*)

Rnd 3: [2 sc in next sc, tr in next sc] around. (*18 sts*)

Rnd 4: [2 sc in next sc, sc in each across to next tr, tr in next tr] around.

Next rnds: Rep last rnd until there are 66 sts.

Next rnds: Work even until piece measures 7 inches from beg. At end of last rnd, **join** (*see Pattern Notes*) in beg sc.

RIBBING

Rnd 1: With size H hook, ch 1, **fphdc** (*see Stitch Guide*) around first st, **bphdc** (*see Stitch Guide*) around next st, [fphdc around next st, bphdc around next st] around, join in beg fphdc.

Rnds 2–4: Ch 1, fphdc around first st, bphdc around next st, [fphdc around next st, bphdc around next st] around, join in beg fphdc. At end of last rnd, fasten off. ■

Comforting Ripple Afghan

DESIGN BY **MELISSA LEAPMAN**

FINISHED SIZE
46 x 67 inches, excluding Fringe

MATERIALS
- Red Heart Super Saver medium (worsted) weight yarn (solid: 7 oz/ 364 yds/198g; fleck: 5 oz/ 260 yds/141g per skein):

  7 skeins #4318 soft white fleck
  2 skeins #321 gold
- Size H/8/5mm crochet hook or size needed to obtain gauge

GAUGE
3 dc groups = 2½ inches; 5 pattern rows = 3 inches

PATTERN NOTES
Chain-6 at beginning of row or round counts as first double crochet and chain-3 unless otherwise stated.

Join with slip stitch as indicated unless otherwise stated.

INSTRUCTIONS
AFGHAN
Row 1: With soft white fleck, ch 217, 3 dc in 7th ch from hook, [sk next 2 chs, 3 dc in next ch] 4 times, sk next 5 chs, [3 dc in next ch, sk next 2 chs] 4 times, *(3 dc, ch 3, 3 dc) in next ch, [sk next 2 chs, 3 dc in next ch] 4 times, sk next 5 chs, [3 dc in next ch, sk next 2 chs] 4 times, rep from * across to last ch, (3 dc, ch 3, dc) in last ch, turn. (70 dc groups, 8 ch sps)

Row 2: Work rem of pattern in ch sps and in sps between dc groups, **ch 6** (see Pattern Notes),
3 dc in first ch sp, 3 dc in each of next 4 sps between dc groups, sk next sp, 3 dc in each of next 4 sps, *(3 dc, ch 2, 3 dc) in next ch sp, 3 dc in each of next 4 sps, sk next sp, 3 dc in each of next 4 sps, rep from * across to last ch sp, (3 dc, ch 3, dc) in last ch sp, turn. Fasten off.

Row 3: **Join** (see Pattern Notes) gold in first st, ch 6, 3 dc in next ch sp, 3 dc in each of next 4 sps, sk next sp, 3 dc in each of next 4 sps, *(3 dc, ch 2, 3 dc) in next ch sp, 3 dc in each of next 4 sps, sk next sp, 3 dc in each of next 4 sps, rep from * across to last ch sp, (3 dc, ch 3, dc) in last ch sp, turn. Fasten off.

Row 4: Join soft white fleck in first st, ch 6, 3 dc in first ch sp, 3 dc in each of next 4 sps between dc groups, sk next sp, 3 dc in each of next 4 sps, *(3 dc, ch 2, 3 dc) in next ch sp, 3 dc in each of next 4 sps, sk next sp, 3 dc in each of next 4 sps, rep from * across to last ch sp, (3 dc, ch 3, dc) in last ch sp, turn.

Row 5: Ch 6, 3 dc in first ch sp, 3 dc in each of next 4 sps between dc groups, sk next sp, 3 dc in each of next 4 sps, *(3 dc, ch 2, 3 dc) in next ch sp, 3 dc in each of next 4 sps, sk next sp, 3 dc in each of next 4 sps, rep from * across to last ch sp, (3 dc, ch 3, dc) in last ch sp, turn. Fasten off.

Next rows: [Rep rows 3–5 consecutively] until piece measures 67 inches. At end of last row, fasten off.

FRINGE
Cut 20 strands gold, each 21 inches long. With all 20 strands held tog, fold in half, insert hook in ch sp, pull fold through, pull all ends through fold, pull to tighten. Trim ends.

Attach Fringe in each point on each short end of Afghan. ∎

love stitches
for Military

Patriotic Granny

DESIGN BY **MICHELE MAKS**

SKILL LEVEL

BEGINNER

FINISHED SIZE
56½ inches square

MATERIALS
- Red Heart Super Saver medium (worsted) weight yarn (7 oz/ 364 yds/198g per skein):
    2 skeins each #319 cherry red and #385 royal
    1 skein #311 white
- Size J/10/6mm crochet hook or size needed to obtain gauge
- Tapestry needle

GAUGE
Each Square = 11 inches square

PATTERN NOTES
Join with slip stitch as indicated unless otherwise stated.

Chain-3 at beginning of round counts as first double crochet unless otherwise stated.

INSTRUCTIONS
AFGHAN
1-COLOR SQUARE
MAKE 13.
Rnd 1: With royal, ch 3, sl st in first ch to form ring, **ch 3** (see Pattern Notes), 2 dc in ring, ch 3, [3 dc in ring, ch 3] 3 times, **join** (see Pattern Notes) in 3rd ch of beg ch-3. (4 ch sps, 12 dc)

Rnd 2: Sl st in each of next 2 sts, sl st in next ch sp, ch 3, (2 dc, ch 3, 3 dc) in same ch sp (corner), ch 1, [(3 dc, ch 3, 3 dc) in next ch sp (corner), ch 1] around, join in 3rd ch of beg ch-3. (4 corners, 8 ch-1 sps)

Rnd 3: Sl st in each of next 2 sts, sl st in next ch sp, ch 3, (2 dc, ch 3, 3 dc) in corner ch sp, *ch 1, sk next 3 sts, 3 dc in next ch-1 sp, ch 1**, (3 dc, ch 3, 3 dc) in next corner ch sp, rep from * around, ending last rep at **, join in 3rd ch of beg ch-3.

Rnds 4–8: Sl st in each of next 2 sts, sl st in first ch sp, ch 3, (2 dc, ch 3, 3 dc) in same corner ch sp, *ch 1, [sk next 3 sts, 3 dc in next ch-1 sp, ch 1] across to next corner ch sp**, (3 dc, ch 3, 3 dc) in corner ch sp, rep from * around, ending last rep at **, join in 3rd ch of beg ch-3. At end of last rnd, fasten off.

2-COLOR SQUARE
MAKE 12.
Rnds 1–3: With cherry red, work rnds 1–3 of 1-Color Square. At end of last rnd, fasten off.

Rnd 4: Join white in any corner ch sp, ch 3, (2 dc, ch 3, 3 dc) in same corner ch sp, *ch 1, [sk next 3 sts, 3 dc in next ch-1 sp, ch 1] across to next corner ch sp**, (3 dc, ch 3, 3 dc) in corner ch sp, rep from * around, ending last rep at **, join in 3rd ch of beg ch-3.

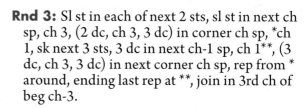

Rnd 5: Sl st in each of next 2 sts, sl st in first ch sp, ch 3, (2 dc, ch 3, 3 dc) in same corner ch sp, *ch 1, [sk next 3 sts, 3 dc in next ch-1 sp, ch 1] across to next corner ch sp**, (3 dc, ch 3, 3 dc) in corner ch sp, rep from * around, ending last rep at **, join in 3rd ch of beg ch-3. Fasten off.

Rnd 6: With cherry red, rep rnd 4.

Rnds 7 & 8: Rep rnd 5. At end of last rnd, fasten off.

STAR
MAKE 5.

Rnd 1: With white, ch 3, sl st in first ch to form ring, ch 3, 11 dc in ring, join in 3rd ch of beg ch-3. *(12 dc)*

Rnd 2: Ch 3, 2 dc in same st, 2 dc in each st around, join in 3rd ch of beg ch-3. *(25 dc)*

Rnd 3: [Ch 7, sl st in 2nd ch from hook, sc in next ch, hdc in next ch, dc in next ch, tr in next ch, dtr in next ch, sk next 4 sts, sl st in next st] around, join in joining sl st of last rnd. Leaving long end, fasten off.

FINISHING

Sew Squares tog, alternating 1-Color and 2-Color Squares, with 1-Color Square in each corner and in center, making 5 rows of 5 Squares.

Sew 1 Star in center of each corner 1-Color Square and in center 1-Color Square.

EDGING

Rnd 1: With RS facing, join white with sc in any corner ch sp, 2 sc in same corner ch sp, sc in each st and in each ch around with 3 sc in each corner ch sp, join in beg sc, turn.

Rnd 2: Ch 1, sc in each st around with 3 sc in each center corner st, join in beg sc. Fasten off. ■

Camo Toe Warmer

DESIGN BY **MICHELE MAKS**

SKILL LEVEL

INTERMEDIATE

FINISHED SIZE

47 x 51 inches

MATERIALS

- Red Heart Super Saver medium (worsted) weight yarn (5 oz/ 244 yds/141g per skein): 5 skeins #971 camouflage
- Size J/10/6mm crochet hook or size needed to obtain gauge
- Tapestry needle
- Stitch markers

GAUGE

12 sts = 4 inches; 12 rows = 6½ inches

PATTERN NOTES

Lapghan and Bottom are made separately and sewn together.

Lapghan is worked from side to side.

Chain-4 at beginning of row or round counts as first double crochet and chain-1 unless otherwise stated.

Chain-3 at beginning of row or round counts as first double crochet unless otherwise stated.

SPECIAL STITCHES

Cluster (cl): Holding last lp of each st on hook, 3 dc in place indicated, yo, pull through all lps on hook.

Cross-stitch (cross-st): Sk 3 sts, dc in next st, ch 1, working behind last dc worked, dc in 2nd sk st.

INSTRUCTIONS
LAPGHAN

Row 1: Ch 150, sc in 2nd ch from hook and in each ch across, turn. *(149 sc)*

Row 2: Ch 4 *(see Pattern Notes)*, sk next st, **cl** *(see Special Stitches)* in next st, [ch 1, **cross-st** *(see Special Stitches)*, ch 1, sk next st, cl in next st] across, ending with ch-1, sk next st, dc in last st, turn.

Row 3: Ch 1, evenly sp 149 sc across, turn. *(149 sc)*

Row 4: Ch 3 *(see Pattern Notes)*, dc in each st across, turn.

Rows 5–12: Ch 3, dc in each st across, turn.

Row 13: Ch 1, sc in each st across, turn.

Rows 14–73: [Rep rows 2–13 consecutively] 5 times.

Rows 74–84: Rep rows 2–12.

EDGING

Rnd 1: Now working in rnds around outer edge in ends of rows and in sts, ch 1, evenly sp sc around with 3 sc in each corner, join with sl st in beg sc, turn.

Rnd 2: Ch 1, sc in each st around with 3 sc in each center corner st, join with sl st in beg sc. Fasten off.

BOTTOM

Row 1: Ch 77, dc in 4th ch from hook (*first 3 chs count as first dc*) and in each ch across, turn. (*75 dc*)

Rows 2–42: Ch 3, dc in each st across, turn.

EDGING

Rnd 1: Now working in rnds around outer edge in ends of rows and in sts, ch 1, evenly sp sc around with 3 sc in each corner, join with sl st in beg sc, turn.

Rnd 2: Ch 1, sc in each st around with 3 sc in each center corner st, join with sl st in beg sc. Fasten off.

ASSEMBLY

Fold Lapghan so row 1 and row 84 are tog.
Mark center on 1 side of Lapghan.

Mark center st of Bottom.

Matching marked centers, sew Bottom to Lapghan along each side edge and across marked edge. ∎

Stars & Stripes

DESIGN BY **BARBARA ROY**

SKILL LEVEL

EASY

FINISHED SIZE
45 x 61 inches

MATERIALS
- Red Heart Super Saver medium (worsted) weight yarn (7 oz/ 364 yds/198g per skein):
  3 skeins each #319 cherry red and #311 white
  2 skeins #387 soft navy
- Size F/5/3.75mm crochet hook or size needed to obtain gauge
- Tapestry needle

GAUGE
16 sc = 4½ inches; 4 sc rows= 1 inch

PATTERN NOTE
Join with slip stitch as indicated unless otherwise stated.

INSTRUCTIONS
AFGHAN
PANEL
MAKE 5.
Row 1 (RS): With cherry red, ch 182, sc in 2nd ch from hook and in each ch across, turn. *(181 sc)*

Row 2: Ch 1, sc in each sc across, turn.

Rows 3–6: Ch 1, sc in each sc across, turn. At the end of last row, fasten off.

Row 7: Join white with sc in first sc, sc in each sc across, turn.

Rows 8–12: Ch 1, sc in each sc across, turn. At the end of last row, fasten off.

Row 13: Join cherry red with sc in first sc, sc in each sc across, turn.

Rows 14–18: Ch 1, sc in each sc across, turn. At the end of last row, fasten off.

Rows 19–30: Rep rows 7–18. At end of last row, fasten off. *(181 sc)*

PANEL EDGING
Rnd 1: With RS facing, join soft navy with sc in last st of row 30, sc in each st across to last st, 3 sc in last st, sc in end of each row across, working in starting ch on opposite side of row 1, 3 sc in first ch, sc in each ch across with 3 sc in last ch, sc in end of each row across to first st of row 30, 2 sc in same st as beg sc, **join** *(see Pattern Notes)* in beg sc, **do not turn**.

Rnd 2: Ch 1, sc in each sc around outer edge of Panel, working 3 sc in center st of each corner, join in beg sc. Fasten off.

PANEL POINT
MAKE 1 ON EACH END OF EACH PANEL.
Row 1: With RS facing, working on end of Panel in **back lps** *(see Stitch Guide)* for this row only, join soft navy with sc in center sc of 3-sc group, sc in each of next 33 sc, turn. *(34 sc)*

Rows 2–16: Ch 1, **sc dec** *(see Stitch Guide)* in first 2 sc, sc in each sc across to last 2 sts, sc dec in last 2 sts, turn. *(4 sc)*

Row 17: Ch 1, sc in each of first 2 sc, sc dec in last 2 sc, turn. *(3 sc)*

Row 18: Ch 1, sc in first st, sc dec in last 2 sts, turn. *(2 sc)*

Row 19: Ch 1, sc dec in next 2 sts. Fasten off. *(1 sc)*

STAR
MAKE 10.
Rnd 1: With white, ch 2, 10 sc in 2nd ch from hook, join in beg sc. *(10 sc)*

Rnd 2: Ch 1, sc in first sc, 2 sc in next sc, [sc in next sc, 2 sc in next sc] around, join in beg sc. *(15 sc)*

Rnd 3: [Ch 6, sl st in 2nd ch from hook, sc in next ch, hdc in next ch, dc in each of next 2 chs, sk next 2 sc of rnd 2, sl st in next sc of rnd 2] 5 times, leaving long end, fasten off. *(5 points)*

Sew 1 Star centered to rows 2–16 of each Panel Point.

ASSEMBLY
With long end of soft navy, leaving all Panel Points unsewn, sew sides of Panels tog side by side.

AFGHAN EDGING
Rnd 1: With RS facing, join soft navy with sc in any st on outer edge, sc around outer edge, working 3 sc in each st of each outer point and at each corner, sk 2 center sts between each inner point to form indent, join in beg sc, **do not turn.**

Rnd 2: Ch 1, sc in each sc around, working 3 sc in each st of each outer point and at each corner, sk 2 center sts between each inner point to form indent, join in beg sc, **do not turn.**

Rnd 3: Sl st in each st around. Fasten off. ∎

Military
Rectangles

DESIGN BY **MICHELE MAKS**

RECTANGLE NO. 1
SKILL LEVEL

EASY

FINISHED SIZE
6 x 9 inches

MATERIALS
- Red Heart Super Saver medium (worsted) weight yarn (7 oz/ 364 yds/198g per skein): 1 oz/50 yds/28g #319 cherry red
- Size J/10/6mm crochet hook or size needed to obtain gauge

GAUGE
12 sts = 4 inches; 8 pattern rows = 3 inches

INSTRUCTIONS
RECTANGLE
Row 1: Ch 19, sc in 2nd ch from hook, dc in next ch, [sc in next ch, dc in next ch] across, turn. *(18 sts)*

Row 2: Ch 1, sc in first st, dc in next st, [sc in next dc, dc in next sc] across, turn.

Next rows: Rep row 2 until piece measures 9 inches. At end of last row, **do not fasten off**.

RECTANGLE NO. 2
SKILL LEVEL

EASY

FINISHED SIZE
6 x 9 inches

MATERIALS
- Red Heart Super Saver medium (worsted) weight yarn (7 oz/ 364 yds/198g per skein): 1 oz/50 yds/28g #311 white
- Size J/10/6mm crochet hook or size needed to obtain gauge

GAUGE
12 sts = 3½ inches; 10 pattern rows = 3 inches

INSTRUCTIONS
RECTANGLE
Row 1: Ch 19, sc in each of first 2 sts, [dc in each of next 2 sts, sc in each of next 2 sts] across, turn. *(18 sc)*

Row 2: Ch 1, sc in each st across, turn.

Row 3: Ch 3, sk first st, dc in next st, [sc in each of next 2 sts, dc in each of next 2 sts] across, turn.

Row 4: Ch 1, sc in each st across to beg ch-3, sc in 3rd ch of beg ch-3, turn.

Row 5: Ch 1, sc in each of first 2 sts, [dc in each of next 2 sts, sc in each of next 2 sts] across, turn.

Next rows: [Rep rows 2–5 consecutively] until piece measures 9 inches from beg. Fasten off at end of last row.

EDGING

With RS facing, work sc evenly spaced in ends of rows along 1 long edge of Rectangle. Rep on rem long edge of Rectangle.

RECTANGLE NO. 3
SKILL LEVEL

EASY

FINISHED SIZE

6½ x 9 inches, including edging

MATERIALS

- Red Heart Super Saver medium (worsted) weight yarn (7 oz/ 364 yds/198g per skein):
    1 oz/50 yds/28g #385 royal
- Size J/10/6mm crochet hook or size needed to obtain gauge

GAUGE

12 sts = 3⅜ inches; 16 pattern rows = 3¾ inches

PATTERN NOTES

Chain-3 at beginning of row or round counts as first double crochet unless otherwise stated.

Chain-2 at beginning of row or round counts as first half double crochet unless otherwise stated.

For donation purposes, do not work edging.

INSTRUCTIONS
RECTANGLE

Row 1: Ch 19, sc in 2nd ch from hook and in each ch across, turn. *(18 sc)*

Row 2: Ch 3 *(see Pattern Notes),* dc in each st across, turn.

Row 3: Ch 2 *(see Pattern Notes),* hdc in next st, [**fpdc** *(see Stitch Guide)* around each of next 2 sts, hdc in each of next 2 sts] across, turn.

Row 4: Ch 3, dc in each st across, turn.

Row 5: Ch 2, hdc in each of first 3 sts, [fpdc around each of next 2 sts, hdc in each of next 2 sts] across, ending with hdc in each of last 2 sts, turn.

Next rows: [Rep rows 2–5 consecutively] until piece measures 9 inches from beg. Fasten off at end of last row.

EDGING

Row 1: With RS facing, work sc evenly spaced in ends of rows along 1 long edge of Rectangle, turn.

Row 2: Ch 1, sc in each sc across, fasten off.

Rep Edging on rem long edge of Rectangle. ∎

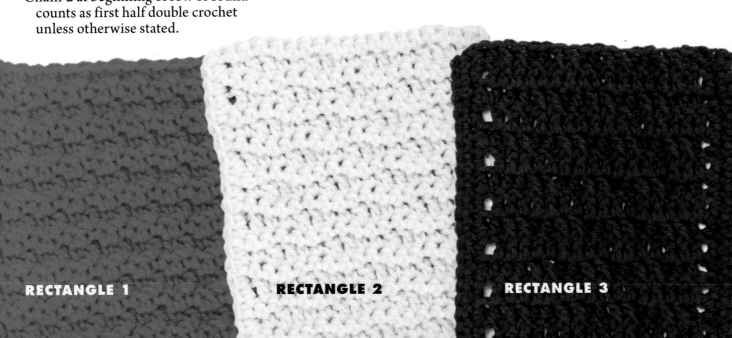

RECTANGLE 1   RECTANGLE 2   RECTANGLE 3

love stitches
for Animals

Pet **Blankets**

DESIGN BY **MICHELE MAKS**

SKILL LEVEL

EASY

FINISHED SIZES

Instructions given for 18 inches square *(small)*;
changes for 25½ x 27 inches *(medium)* and
36 inches square *(large)* are in [ ].

MATERIALS

- TLC Essentials medium (worsted)
  weight yarn (solids: 6 oz/
  312 yds/170g/multis: 4½ oz/
  245 yds/127g per skein)
    1 skein each #2991 sedona multi *(A)*
    and #2335 taupe *(B)* *(small)*
    3 skeins #2332 linen *(B)* *(large)*
    2 skeins #2982 choco cherry multi
    (A) *(large)*
- Red Heart Super Saver medium (worsted)
  weight yarn (solids: 7 oz/364 yds/198g;
  prints: 5 oz/244 yds/141g per skein):
    2 skeins #972 pink camo *(A)* *(medium)*
    1 skein #373 petal pink *(B)* *(medium)*
- Size J/10/6mm crochet hook
  or size needed to obtain gauge
- Tapestry needle

GAUGE

12 sc = 4 inches; 15 sc rows = 4 inches

INSTRUCTIONS
BLANKET
SQUARE
MAKE 5 [5, 5] EACH OF A AND 4 [4, 4] EACH OF B.

Row 1: Ch 19 [28, 37], sc in 2nd ch from hook
and in each ch across, turn. *(18 [27, 36] sc)*

Rows 2–22 [2–32, 2–45]: Ch 1, sc in each st
across, turn. At end of last row, fasten off.

FINISHING

Alternating Squares, using A, sew Squares tog in
3 rows of 3 Squares.

With A, work overhand sts around entire outer
edge in each st and in end of each row around. ∎

Catnip Mouse

DESIGN BY **MICHELE MAKS**

SKILL LEVEL

EASY

FINISHED SIZE
7½ inches long, including tail

MATERIALS
- Lion Brand Lion Cotton medium (worsted) weight yarn (5 oz/ 236 yds/140g per ball)
  1 ball each #152 espresso and #136 clove *(will make several)*
- Size H/8/5mm crochet hook or size needed to obtain gauge
- Fiberfill
- Small muslin bag for catnip
- Catnip

4

MEDIUM

GAUGE
14 sc = 4 inches; 16 sc rows = 4 inches

SPECIAL STITCH
Cluster (cl): Holding back last lp of each st on hook, 3 dc in place indicated, yo, pull through all lps on hook.

INSTRUCTIONS
MOUSE
BODY
Row 1: With coffee, ch 2, 4 sc in 2nd ch from hook, turn. *(4 sc)*

Rows 2 & 3: 2 sc in each st across, turn. *(16 sc at end of last row)*

Rows 4–9: Ch 1, sc in each st across, turn.

Rows 10–15: Ch 1, **sc dec** *(see Stitch Guide)* in first 2 sts, sc in each st across, ending with sc dec in last 2 sts, turn. *(4 sc at end of last row)*

Row 16: Ch 1, sc dec in first 2 sts, sc dec in last 2 sts, turn. *(2 sc)*

Row 17: Ch 1, sc dec in next 2 sts, **changing colors** *(see Stitch Guide)* to espresso in st, turn. *(1 sc)*

Row 18: Ch 3, **cl** *(see Special Stitch)* in same st *(nose)*. Fasten off.

TAIL
Join coffee in ch on opposite side of row 1 of Body, ch 12, sl st in 2nd ch from hook and in each ch across. Fasten off.

EAR
MAKE 2.
Row 1: With espresso, ch 2, sc in 2nd ch from hook, turn. *(1 sc)*

Row 2: Ch 1, 8 sc in sc. Fasten off.

FINISHING
Sew Ears to Mouse as shown in photo.

Turn nose under in half and sew ends of rows on body tog, stuffing with fiberfill and muslin bag of catnip before closing. ∎

love stitches for the Displaced

Women's & Men's
Hat, Scarf & Mittens
DESIGN BY **GLENDA WINKLEMAN**

SKILL LEVEL

INTERMEDIATE

FINISHED SIZES
Instructions given for women's; changes for
men's are in [ ].
Hat: One size fits most
Mittens: One size fits most

FINISHED GARMENT MEASUREMENTS
Women's Scarf: 5 x 66 inches
Men's Scarf: 6 x 68 inches

MATERIALS
- Red Heart Super Saver medium
  (worsted) weight yarn (solids:
  7 oz/364 yds/198g; prints: 5 oz/
  244 yds/141g per skein):
    3 skeins #631 light sage for women's
    5 skeins #305 aspen print for men's
- Sizes H/8/5mm and I/9/5.5mm crochet
  hooks or size needed to obtain gauge
- Tapestry needle
- ⅛-inch braided elastic: 2 yds
- Stitch marker

GAUGE
Size I hook: 16 sts = 4 inches; 14 rows = 4 inches

44

PATTERN NOTES

Work in continuous rounds; do not turn or join unless otherwise stated.

Mark first stitch of each round.

Join with slip stitch as indicated unless otherwise stated.

INSTRUCTIONS
HAT

Rnd 1: Beg at top, with size I hook, ch 2, 6 sc in 2nd ch from hook, **do not join** (see Pattern Notes). (6 sc)

Rnd 2: 2 sc in each st around. (12 sc)

Rnds 3 & 4: [Sc in each of next 2 sts, working across sts just worked, sc in same st as first sc just worked] around. (27 sc at end of last rnd)

Rnd 5: [Sc in each of next 2 sts, working across sts just worked, sc in same st as first sc just worked] around to last st, sc in last st. (40 sc)

Rnd 6: [Sk next st, sc in next st, working across st just worked, sc in st just sk] around. (60 sc)

Rnd 7: Rep rnd 3.

Rnd 8: Rep rnd 6.

WOMEN'S SIZE ONLY

Rnd 9: [Sc in each of next 2 sts, working across sts just worked, sc in same st as first sc just worked, sc in each of next 2 sts] around. (75 sc)

Rnd 10: [Sk next st, sc in next st, working across st just worked, sc in st just sk] around to last st, 2 sc in last st. (76 sc)

MEN'S SIZE ONLY

Rnd [9]: Rep rnd 3. ([90] sc)

Rnd [10]: Rep rnd 6.

ALL SIZES

Rnds 11–27 [11–29]: Rep rnd 6. At end of last rnd, **join** (see Pattern Notes) in beg sc. At end of last rnd, fasten off.

BRIM

Row 1: With size H hook, ch 9 [11], sc in 2nd ch from hook and in each ch across, turn. (8 [10] sc)

Rows 2–76 [2–90]: Working in **back lps** (see Stitch Guide), ch 1, sc in each st across, turn. At end of last row, fasten off.

FINISHING

Sew last row of Brim to starting ch on opposite side of row 1, forming ring.

Sew ends of rows on 1 side of ring to last rnd of Hat.

SCARF

Row 1: With size I hook, ch 21 [25], sc in 2nd ch from hook, [sk next ch, sc in next ch, working over last sc worked, sc in ch just sk] across, ending with sc in last ch, turn. (20 [24] sc)

Rows 2–231 [2–238]: Ch 1, sc in first st, sk next st, sc in next st, working over last sc worked, sc in st just sk] across, ending with sc in last st. At end of last row, fasten off.

MITTEN
MAKE 2.

Row 1: With size H [I] hook, ch 84, sc in 2nd ch from hook and in each of next 9 chs, sl st in each of next 2 chs, *[sk next ch, sc in next ch, working over sc just worked, sc in ch just sk] 14 times*, sl st in each of next 3 chs, rep between * once, sl st in each of next 2 chs, sc in each of last 10 chs, turn.

Row 2: Ch 1, sc in back lp of each of first 10 sts, sc in both lps of each of next 2 sl sts, *[sk next st, sc in next st, working over st just worked, sc in st just sk] 14 times*, sl st in each of next 3 sl sts, rep between * once, sc in each of next 2 sl sts, sc in back lp of each of last 10 sts, turn.

Row 3: Ch 1, sc in back lp of each of first 10 sts, sl st in each of next 2 sts, *[sk next st, sc in next st, working over st just worked, sc in st just sk] 14 times*, sl st in each of next 3 sl sts, rep between * once, sc in each of next 2 sl sts, sc in back lp of each of last 10 sts, turn.

Rows 4–13: [Rep rows 2 and 3 alternately] 5 times.

Row 14: Rep row 2.

THUMB

Row 15: Ch 1, sc in back lp of each of first 10 sts, sl st in each of next 2 sts, *[sk next st, sc in next st, working over st just worked, sc in st just sk]* 6 times, ch 18, sk next 36 sts, sc in next st, working over last st worked, sc in last st just sk, rep between * 5 times, sl st in each of next 2 sts, sc in back lp of each of last 10 sts, turn.

Row 16: Ch 1, sc in back lp of each of first 10 sts, sc in each of next 2 sl sts, *[sk next st, sc in next st, working over last sc worked, sc in st just sk] 6 times*, working across ch, sc in each of first 8 chs, sl st in each of next 2 chs, sc in each of last 8 chs, rep between * once, sc in each of next 2 sl sts, sc in back lp of each of last 10 sts, turn.

Row 17: Ch 1, sc in back lp of each of first 10 sts, sl st in each of next 2 sl sts, *[sk next st, sc in next st, working over last sc worked, sc in st just sk] 10 times*, sl st in each of next 2 sl sts, rep between * once, sl st in each of next 2 sts, sc in back lp of each of last 10 sts, turn.

Row 18: Ch 1, sc in back lp of each of first 10 sts, sc in each of next 2 sl sts, *[sk next st, sc in next st, working over last sc worked, sc in st just sk] 10 times*, sl st in each of next 2 sl sts, rep between * once, sc in each of next 2 sl sts, sc in back lp of each of last 10 sts, turn.

Row 19: Rep row 17.

Row 20: Rep row 18.

Row 21: Rep row 17. Leaving long end, fasten off.

FINISHING

Fold Mitten in half, sew tog around outer edge, leaving bottom edge open.

Cut 2 pieces of elastic, each 15 inches long.

Weave 1 piece through back lps of 10th st from bottom on WS of Mitten, pull and gather until comfortable to your hand size. Tie ends of elastic tog. Turn RS out. ■

Women's & Men's
Knit-Look
Hat, Scarf & Mittens

DESIGN BY **GLENDA WINKLEMAN**

SKILL LEVEL

INTERMEDIATE

FINISHED SIZES

Instructions given for women's; changes for men's are in [ ].
Hat: One size fits most
Mittens: One size fits most

FINISHED GARMENT MEASUREMENTS

Women's Scarf: 5½ x 73 inches
Men's Scarf: 6 x 72 inches

MATERIALS
- TLC Essentials medium (worsted) weight yarn (solids: 6 oz/ 312 yds/170g; multis: 4½ oz/ 245 yds/127g per skein):
    5 skeins #2991 sedona multi for women's
    3 skeins #2919 barn red for men's
    1 skein #2332 linen
- Size J/10/6mm afghan crochet hook or size needed to obtain gauge
- Sizes H/8/5mm and I/9/5.5mm crochet hooks
- Tapestry needle
- Stitch marker

GAUGE

Size J hook: 15 knit sts = 4 inches; 19 knit rows = 4 inches

PATTERN NOTE

Join with slip stitch as indicated unless otherwise stated.

SPECIAL STITCHES

Work loops off hook (work lps off hook): Yo, pull through 1 lp on hook (*see A of Fig. 1*), [yo, pull through 2 lps on hook] across, leaving 1 lp on hook at end of row (*see B of Fig. 1*), last lp on hook counts as first lp of next row.

Fig. 1
Work Loops Off Hook

Knit stitch (knit st): With yarn in back, insert hook from front to back (*see Fig. 2*), pull lp through.

Fig. 2
Knit Stitch

Knit stitch decrease (knit st dec): Insert hook under next vertical bar and continue from front to back between both vertical stands of next st, yo, pull through both sts.

Knit stitch increase (knit st inc): Insert hook under horizontal bars between lp on hook and next vertical st, yo, pull lp through st, keeping lp on hook.

INSTRUCTIONS
HAT

Row 1: Beg at bottom with size J hook, ch 88 [92], holding all lps on hook, pull up lp in 2nd ch from hook and in each ch across (*you will have 88 [92] lps on hook*), **work lps off hook** (*see Special Stitches*) across.

Rows 2–16 [2–19]: Work **knit st** (*see Special Stitches*) across, work lps off hook.

Row 17 [20]: Knit st in each of next 3 sts, **knit st dec** (*see Special Stitches*) in next 2 sts, [knit st in each of next 4 sts, knit st dec in next 2 sts] across to last 4 [2] sts, knit st in each st across (*74 [77] lps on hook*), work lps off hook.

Row 18 [21]: Knit st across, work lps off hook.

Row 19 [22]: Knit st in each of next 2 sts, knit st dec in next 2 sts, [knit st in each of next 3 sts, knit st dec in next st] across to last 4 [2] sts, knit st in each st across (*60 [62] lps on hook*), work lps off hook.

Row 20 [23]: Knit st in each st across, work lps off hook.

Row 21 [24]: Knit st in next st, knit st dec in next 2 sts, [knit st in each of next 2 sts, knit st dec in next 2 sts] across to last 4 [2] sts, knit st across *(46 [47] lps on hook)*, work lps off hook.

Rows 22 & 23 [25 & 26]: Knit st in each st across, work off lps.

Row 24 [27]: Knit st in next st, knit st dec in next 2 sts, [knit st in each of next 2 sts, knit st dec in next 2 sts] across to last 2 [3] sts, knit st in each st across *(35 [36] lps on hook)*, work lps off hook.

Rows 25 & 26 [28 & 29]: Knit st across, work lps off hook.

Row 27 [30]: Knit st in next st, knit st dec in next 2 sts, [knit st in each of next 2 sts, knit st dec in next 2 sts] across to last 3 [4] sts, knit st in each st across *(27 [28] lps on hook)*, work lps off hook.

Row 28 [31]: Rep row 27 [30]. *(21 [22] lps on hook)*

Row 29 [32]: Knit st dec in first 2 sts, [knit st in next st, knit st dec in next 2 sts] across to last st, knit st in last 0 [1] st *(14 [15] lps on hook)*, work lps off hook.

Row 30 [33]: [Knit st dec in next 2 sts] 6 times, knit st in each of last 1 [2] st(s) *(8 [9] lps on hook)*, work lps off hook.

Row 31 [34]: [Knit st dec in next 2 sts] 3 times, knit st in each st across *(5 [6] lps on hook)*, work lps off hook.

Row 32 [35]: Insert hook under next 4 [5] vertical bars, yo, pull lp through all lps on hook. Fasten off.

BRIM
WOMEN'S SIZE ONLY
Row 1: With RS facing and working in starting ch on opposite side of row 1, with size H hook, join with sc in first ch, sc in each ch across, turn. *(88 sc)*

Rows 2–7: Ch 1, sc in each st across. At end of last row, **do not turn**.

Row 8: Ch 1, working from left to right, **reverse sc** *(see Fig. 3)* in each st across. Leaving long end, fasten off.

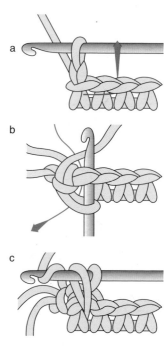

Fig. 3
Reverse Single Crochet

FINISHING
With RS tog, sew ends of rows tog from bottom to top.

Turn RS out.

MEN'S SIZE ONLY
Row [1]: With RS facing, working in starting ch on opposite side of row 1, with size H hook, join linen with sc in first ch, sc in each ch across, turn. Fasten off. *(92 sc)*

Row [2]: Join barn red with sc in first st, sc in each st across, turn,

Row [3]: Ch 1, sc in each st across, turn. Fasten off.

Row [4]: Join linen with sc in first st, sc in each st across, turn. Fasten off.

Row [5]: Join barn red with sc in first st, sc in each st across, turn. Leaving long end, fasten off.

FINISHING
With RS tog, sew ends of rows tog from bottom to top.

Turn RS out.

WOMEN'S SCARF
Row 1: With size J hook, ch 21, pull up lp in 2nd ch from hook and in each ch across (*21 lps on hook*), **work lps off hook** (*see Special Stitches*).

Rows 2–348: **Knit st** (*see Special Stitches*) across, work lps off hook.

Row 349: Sl st in each st across. Fasten off.

FRINGE
Cut 84 strands, each 16 inches in length. With 2 strands held tog, fold in half, pull fold through st, pull ends through fold. Pull to tighten.

Attach Fringe in each st across each short end of Scarf.

MEN'S SCARF
Row 1: With size J hook and linen, ch 23, pull up lp in 2nd ch from hook and in each ch across (*23 lps on hook*), **work lps off hook** (*see Special Stitches*).

Row 2: With barn red, **knit st** (*see Special Stitches*) in each st across, work lps off hook.

Rows 3: With linen, knit st in each st across, work lps off hook.

Row 4: With barn red, knit st in each st across, work lps off hook.

Rows 5–10: Knit st in each st across, work lps off hook.

Row 11: With linen, knit st in each st across, work lps off hook.

Row 12: With barn red, knit st in each st across, work lps off hook.

Row 13: With linen, knit st in each st across, work lps off hook.

Rows 14–343: [Rep rows 4–13 consecutively] 33 times.

Row 344: Sl st in each st across. Fasten off.

FRINGE
Cut 92 strands, each 16 inches in length. With 2 strands held tog, fold in half, pull fold through st, pull ends through fold. Pull to tighten.

Attach Fringe in each st across each short end of Scarf.

MITTEN
MAKE 2.
FRONT
Row 1: With size J hook and sedona [barn red], ch 13 [19], pull up lp in 2nd ch from hook and in each ch across (*13 [19] lps on hook*), **work lps off hook** (*see Special Stitches*).

Row 2: **Knit st** (*see Special Stitches*) across, work lps off hook.

Row 3: **Knit st inc** (*see Special Stitches*), knit st in each of next 12 [18] sts (*14 [20] lps on hook*), work lps off hook.

Row 4: Knit st across, work lps off hook.

Row 5: Knit st inc, knit st in each st across, (*15 [21] lps on hook*), work lps off hook.

Row 6: Knit st in each of next 13 [19] sts, knit st inc, knit st in last st (*16 [22] lps on hook*), work lps off hook.

Row 7: Knit st inc, knit st in each st across, (*17 [23] lps on hook*), work lps off hook.

Row 8: Knit st across, work lps off hook.

Row 9: Knit st inc, knit st in each st across, (*18 [24] lps on hook*), work lps off hook.

Row 10: Knit st across, work lps off hook.

Row 11: Knit st inc, knit st in each st across, (*19 [25] lps on hook*), work lps off hook.

Rows 12–14: Knit st across, work lps off hook.

Row 15: Knit st inc, knit st in each st across, *(20 [26] lps on hook)*, work lps off hook.

Row 16: Knit st in each st across, work lps off hook.

THUMB

Row 17: Place st marker in 7th [9th] st from hook counting first lp on hook as first st, knit st in each of next 5 [7] sts *(6 [8] lps on hook)*, work lps off hook.

Rows 18–23: Knit st in each st across, work lps off hook.

WOMEN'S ONLY

Row 24: [**Knit st dec** *(see Special Stitches)* in next 2 sts] twice, knit st in last st *(4 lps on hook)*, yo, pull through all lps on hook. Fasten off.

MEN'S ONLY

Row [24]: [**Knit st dec** *(see Special Stitches)* in next 2 sts] 3 times, knit st in last st *([5] lps on hook)*, work lps off hook.

Row [25]: [Knit st dec in next 2 sts] twice, *([3] lps on hook)*, yo, pull through all lps on hook. Fasten off.

PALM

Row 17: Join sedona [barn red] in first st to left of marker on row 16, sk marked st, knit st in each of next 13 [17] sts, work lps off hook.

Rows 18–32: Knit st in each st across, work lps off hook.

Row 33 [37]: [Knit st dec in next 2 sts] 2 [3] times, knit st in each of next 3 sts, knit st dec in next 2 sts] 2 [3] times, knit st in last st *(9 [11] lps on hook)*, work lps off hook.

Row 34 [38]: Knit st dec in next 2 sts, knit st in each of next 3 [5] sts, knit st dec in next 2 sts, knit st in last st *(7 [9] lps on hook)*, work lps off hook.

Row 35 [39]: Knit st dec in next 2 sts, knit st in next 1 [3] sts, knit st dec in next 2 sts, knit st in last st *(5 [7] lps on hook)*, work lps off hook. Fasten off.

BACK

Row 1: With size J hook and sedona [barn red], ch 13 [19], pull up lp in 2nd ch from hook and in each ch across *(13 [19] lps on hook)*, work lps off hook.

Row 2: Knit st across, work lps off hook.

Row 3: Knit st in each of next 11 [17] sts, knit st inc, knit st in last st *(14 [20] lps on hook)*, work lps off hook.

Row 4: Knit st in each st across, work lps off hook.

Row 5: Knit st in each of next 12 [18] sts, knit st inc, knit st in last st *(15 [21] lps on hook)*, work lps off hook.

Row 6: Knit st inc, knit st in each of next 14 [20] sts, *(16 [22] lps on hook)*, work lps off hook.

Rows 7 & 8: Knit st in each st across, work lps off hook.

Row 9: Knit st in each of next 14 [20] sts, knit st inc, knit st in last st *(17 [23] lps on hook)*, work lps off hook.

Row 10: Knit st in each st across, work lps off hook.

Row 11: Knit st in each of next 15 [21] sts, knit st inc, knit st in last st *(18 [24] lps on hook)*, work lps off hook.

Row 12: Knit st in each st across, work lps off hook.

Row 13: Knit st in each of next 16 [22] sts, knit st inc, knit st in last st *(19 [25] lps on hook)*, work lps off hook.

Row 14: Knit st in each st across, work lps off hook.

Row 15: Knit st in each of next 17 [23] sts, knit st inc, knit st in last st *(20 [26] lps on hook)*, work lps off hook.

Row 16: Knit st in each st across, work lps off hook.

Row 17: Place st marker in 14th [18th] st from hook, counting first lp on hook as first st, knit st in each of next 12 [16] sts *(13 [17] lps on hook)*, work lps off hook.

Rows 18–32: Knit st in each st across, work lps off hook.

Row 33 [37]: [Knit st dec in next 2 sts] 2 [3] times, knit st in each of next 3 sts, [knit st dec in next 2 sts] 2 [3] times, knit st in last st *(9 [11] lps on hook)*, work lps off hook.

Row 34 [38]: Knit st dec in next 2 sts, knit st in each of next 3 [5] sts, knit st dec in next 2 sts, knit st in last st *(7 [9] lps on hook)*, work lps off hook.

Row 35 [39]: Knit st dec in next 2 sts, knit st in next 1 [3] st(s), knit st dec in next 2 sts, knit st in last st *(5 [7] lps on hook)*, work lps off hook. Fasten off.

THUMB

Row 17: Join sedona [barn red] in first st on row 16 to left of marker, sk marked st, knit st in each of next 6 [8] sts, *(6 [8] lps on hook)*, work lps off hook.

Rows 18–23: Knit st in each st across, work lps off hook.

WOMEN'S ONLY

Row 24: [Knit st dec] twice, knit st in last st *(4 lps on hook)*, yo, pull through all lps on hook. Fasten off.

MEN'S ONLY

Row [24]: [Knit dec in next 2 sts] 3 times, knit st in last st *([5] lps on hook)*, work lps off hook.

Row [25]: [Knit st dec in next 2 sts] twice *([3] lps on hook)*, yo, pull through all lps on hook. Fasten off.

ASSEMBLY

Place Front and Back pieces RS tog, sew tog around, leaving bottom edge of Mitten open.

Turn RS out.

WOMEN'S CUFF

Rnd 1: Working in starting ch on opposite side of row 1 on Front and Back, with RS facing, join sedonia with sc at seam, evenly sp 25 sc around, **join** *(see Pattern Note)* in beg sc. *(26 sc)*

Rnds 2–5: Ch 1, sc in each st around, join in beg sc. At end of last rnd, fasten off.

MEN'S CUFF

Rnd [1]: Working in starting ch on opposite side of row 1 on Front and Back, with RS facing, join barn red with sc at seam, evenly sp [29] sc around, **join** *(see Pattern Note)* in beg sc. Fasten off. *([30] sc)*

Rnd [2]: Join linen with sc in first st, sc in each st around, join in beg sc. Fasten off.

Rnd [3]: Join barn red with sc in first st, sc in each st around, join in beg sc.

Rnd [4]: Ch 1, sc in each st around, join in beg sc. Fasten off.

Rnd [5]: Join linen with sc in first st, sc in each st around, join in beg sc. Fasten off.

Rnd [6]: Join barn red with sc in first st, sc in each st around, join in beg sc. Fasten off. ∎

Warm Up America Squares

DESIGNS BY **MICHELE MAKS**

SQUARE 1
SKILL LEVEL

EASY

FINISHED SIZE
8 x 9½ inches, including edging

MATERIALS
- Red Heart Super Saver medium (worsted) weight yarn (7 oz/ 364 yds/198g per skein): 1 oz/50 yds/28g each #718 shocking pink, #254 pumpkin and #327 light coral
- Size J/10/6mm crochet hook

GAUGE
12 sts = 4 inches; 8 pattern rows = 3 inches

PATTERN NOTE
Chain-2 at beginning of row or round **does not** count as first half double crochet unless otherwise stated.

INSTRUCTIONS
SECTION
Row 1: With pumpkin, ch 24, sc in 2nd ch from hook, *ch 3, sk next 3 chs**, dc in each of next 3 chs, rep from * across, ending last rep at **, dc in last ch, **changing colors** (*see Stitch Guide*) to shocking pink in last st, turn. **Do not fasten off pumpkin and do not carry yarn across.**

Row 2: Ch 2, hdc in first st, *working over ch sp on last row, dc in each of next 3 sk chs**, ch 3, sk next 3 sts, rep from * across, ending last rep at **, hdc in last st, changing to light coral in last st, turn. **Do not fasten off and do not carry yarn.**

Row 3: Ch 2, hdc in first st, *ch 3, sk next 3 sts**, working over ch sp, dc in each of next 3 sk sts on row before last, rep from * across, ending last rep **, dc in last st, changing to dropped pumpkin, turn.

Row 4: Ch 2, hdc in first st, *working over ch sp on last row, dc in each of next 3 sk sts**, ch 3, sk next 3 sts, rep from * across, ending last rep at **, hdc in last st changing to light coral in last st, turn.

Next rows: Rep rows 3 and 4, alternately in established color sequence until piece measures 8¾ inches from beg, ending with row 3.

Last row: Ch 2, hdc in first st, *working over ch sp of last row, dc in each of 3 sk sts**, sc in each of next 3 sts, rep from * across, ending last rep at **, hdc in last st. Fasten off.

EDGING

Working around outer edge in ends of rows and in sts, join pumpkin with sc in any corner, evenly sp sc around with 3 sc in each corner, join with sl st in beg sc. Fasten off.

SQUARE 2
SKILL LEVEL

EASY

FINISHED SIZE

7½ x 9 inches, including edging

MATERIALS

- Red Heart Super Saver medium (worsted) weight yarn (7 oz/ 364 yds/198g per skein):
  1 oz/50 yds/28g each #672 spring green, #885 delft blue and #512 turqua
- Size J/10/6mm crochet hook

4 MEDIUM

GAUGE

19 sts = 7 inches; 11 rows = 2½ inches

INSTRUCTIONS
SECTION

Row 1: With delft blue, ch 20, sc in 2nd ch from hook and in each ch across, turn. *(19 sc)*

Row 2: Ch 1, sc in each st across, **changing colors** *(see Stitch Guide)* to spring green in last st, turn. **Do not fasten off or carry yarn behind work.**

Row 3: Ch 1, sc in first st, [working over st on last row, sc in st 2 rows below, sc in next st] across, turn.

Row 4: Ch 1, sc in each st across, changing to turqua in last st. **Do not fasten off or carry yarn behind work.**

Row 5: Ch 1, sc in each of first 2 sts, [working over st on last row, sc in next st 2 rows below, sc in next st] across, ending with sc in last st, turn.

Row 6: Ch 1, sc in each st across, changing to delft blue in last st, turn.

Next rows: [Rep rows 3–6 consecutively], changing colors in established sequence until there are 19 color changes, ending with row 3 and spring green. At end of last row, fasten off.

EDGING

Working around outer edge in ends of rows and in sts, with RS facing, join turqua with sc in first st, 2 sc in same st, evenly sc around so piece lies flat, with 3 sc in each corner, join with sl st in beg sc. Fasten off.

SQUARE 3
SKILL LEVEL

EASY

FINISHED SIZE
8 x 9 inches, including edging

MATERIALS
- Red Heart Super Saver medium (worsted) weight yarn (7 oz/ 364 yds/198g per skein): 1 oz/50 yds/28g each #365 coffee, #334 buff and #332 ranch red
- Size J/10/6mm crochet hook

GAUGE
25 sts = 7 inches; 15 rows = 9 inches

PATTERN NOTES
Join with slip stitch as indicated unless otherwise stated.

Chain-3 at beginning of row or round counts as first double crochet unless otherwise stated.

INSTRUCTIONS
SECTION
Row 1: With buff, ch 26, sc in 2nd ch from hook, [sk next 2 chs, 5 dc in next ch, sk next 2 chs, sc in next ch] across, turn. Fasten off. *(25 sts)*

Row 2: **Join** *(see Pattern Notes)* ranch red in first st, **ch 3** *(see Pattern Notes)*, 2 dc in same st, sk next 2 dc, sc in next dc, sk next 2 dc, [5 dc in next sc, sk next 2 dc, sc in next sc, sk next 2 dc] across, ending with 3 dc in last sc, turn.

Row 3: Ch 1, sc in first st, [sk next 2 dc, 5 dc in next sc, sk next 2 dc, sc in next dc] across, turn. Fasten off.

Next rows: [Rep rows 2 and 3 alternately] in color sequences of buff, coffee, buff, ranch red, buff, coffee, ending with row 2 and buff.

Last row: Ch 1, sc in first st, [hdc in each of next 2 dc, dc in next sc, hdc in each of next 2 dc, sc in next dc] across, **do not turn.**

EDGING
Working around outer edge and in ends of rows, ch 1, evenly sp sc around so piece lies flat with 3 sc in each corner, join in beg sc. Fasten off. ∎

Circle in the Square

DESIGN BY MARTY MILLER

SKILL LEVEL
INTERMEDIATE

FINISHED SIZE
55 x 66 inches

MATERIALS
- Red Heart Collage medium (worsted) weight yarn (3½ oz/ 218 yds/100g per skein):
  9 skeins #2350 blue wave
- Red Heart Super Saver medium (worsted) weight yarn (7 oz/364 yds/198g per skein):
  1 skein each #381 light blue, #347 light periwinkle and #885 delft blue
- Size J/10/6mm crochet hook or size needed to obtain gauge
- Tapestry needle

4 MEDIUM

GAUGE
Square = 10 inches square

PATTERN NOTES
Chain-3 at beginning of row or round counts as first double crochet unless otherwise stated.

Join with slip stitch as indicated unless otherwise stated.

INSTRUCTIONS
AFGHAN
CIRCLE
MAKE 10 EACH LIGHT BLUE, LIGHT PERIWINKLE AND DELFT BLUE.

Rnd 1: Ch 4, 11 dc in 4th ch from hook, **join** (see Pattern Notes) in 3rd ch of beg ch-3. (12 dc)

Rnd 2: **Ch 3** (see Pattern Notes), dc in same st, 2 dc in each st around, join in 3rd ch of beg ch-3. (24 dc)

Rnd 3: Ch 3, dc in same st, dc in next st, [2 dc in next st, dc in next st] around, join in 3rd ch of beg ch-3. Fasten off. (36 dc)

SQUARING CIRCLES
Rnd 1: Join blue wave with sc in first st, *hdc in each of next 2 sts, dc in each of next 2 sts, ch 3 (corner), dc in each of next 2 sts, hdc in each of next 2 sts**, sc in next st, rep from * around, ending last rep at **, join in beg sc. (36 sts)

Rnd 2: Ch 3, dc in each of next 4 sts, *(2 tr, ch 3, 2 tr) in next corner ch sp, dc in each st across** to next ch sp, rep from * around, ending last rep at **, join in 3rd ch of beg ch-3. (52 sts)

Rnd 3: Ch 3, *dc in each st across** to corner ch sp, (2 tr, ch 2, 2 tr) in corner ch sp, rep from * around, ending last rep at **, join in 3rd ch of beg ch-3. (68 sts)

Rnd 4: Ch 3, *dc in each st across** to corner ch sp, (2 tr, ch 1, 2 tr) in corner ch sp, rep from * around, ending last rep at **, join in 3rd ch of beg ch-3. (84 sts)

Rnd 5: Ch 3, *dc in each st across** to corner ch sp, (tr, ch 1, tr) in corner ch sp, rep from * around, ending last rep at **, join in 3rd ch of beg ch-3. Fasten off. (92 sts)

Alternating Circle colors, making 6 rows of 5 Squares, join Squares tog beg at bottom right corner.

Join blue wave with sc in top corner of first
Square on right side of row, [ch 1, sc in
corresponding st of first Square on bottom
right of row, ch 1, sc in next st on this Square]
continue in this pattern until end of row.
Fasten off.

Join rem rows and Squares in same manner.

BORDER
Rnd 1: Working around outer edges, join blue
wave in any corner ch sp, sc in each st and in
each ch sp around with 3 sc in each corner ch
sp, join in beg sc.

Rnd 2: Ch 1, working from left to right, **reverse
sc** (*see Fig. 1*) in next st and in each st around,
join in beg reverse sc. Fasten off. ∎

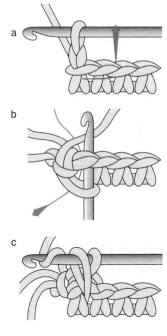

Fig. 1
Reverse Single Crochet

Strips & Blocks Afghan

DESIGN BY MICHELE MAKS

SKILL LEVEL

EASY

FINISHED SIZE
51½ x 57½ inches

MATERIALS
- Red Heart Super Saver medium (worsted) weight yarn (7 oz/ 364 yds/198g per skein):
  3 skeins #389 hunter green
  2 skeins #656 real teal
  1 skein each #385 royal, #885 delft blue, #334 buff, #718 shocking pink, #254 pumpkin, #332 ranch red, #365 coffee, #378 claret, #672 spring green, #512 turqua, #905 magenta and #327 light coral
- Size J/10/6mm crochet hook or size needed to obtain gauge

GAUGE
28 sc = 10 inches; 15 sc rows = 4 inches

PATTERN NOTE
Join with slip stitch as indicted unless otherwise stated.

PATTERN
Row 1: Join color with sc in first st, sc in each st across, turn.

Row 2: Ch 1, sc in each st across, turn.

Row 3: Ch 1, sc in each st across, turn. Fasten off.

INSTRUCTIONS
AFGHAN
STRIP A
MAKE 2.
FIRST BLOCK
Row 1: With real teal, ch 29, sc in 2nd ch from hook and in each ch across, turn. (*28 sc*)

Row 2: Work row 3 of Pattern.

Row 3: With hunter green, work row 1 of Pattern.

Row 4: Work row 3 of Pattern.

Rows 5 & 6: With real teal, work rows 2 and 3 of Pattern.

Rows 7–30: [Rep rows 3–6 consecutively] 6 times.

2ND BLOCK
Row 1: With buff, work row 1 of Pattern.

Rows 2–9: Work row 2 of Pattern.

Row 10: Work row 3 of Pattern.

Rows 11 & 12: With shocking pink, work rows 1 and 3 of Pattern.

Rows 13 & 14: With pumpkin, work rows 1 and 3 of Pattern.

Rows 15–18: Rep rows 11–14 of this Block.

Rows 19 & 20: Rep rows 11 and 12.

Rows 21–30: Rep rows 1–10 of this Block.

3RD BLOCK
Rows 1 & 2: With real teal, work rows 1 and 3 of Pattern.

Row 3: With hunter green, work row 1 of Pattern.

Row 4: Work row 3 of Pattern

Rows 5 & 6: With real teal, work rows 2 and 3 of Pattern.

Rows 7–30: [Rep rows 3–6 of this Block consecutively] 6 times.

4TH BLOCK
Rows 1 & 2: With royal, work rows 1 and 3 of Pattern.

Rows 3 & 4: With delft blue, work rows 1 and 3 of Pattern.

Rows 5–8: Rep rows 1–4 of this Block.

Rows 9 & 10: Rep rows 1 and 2 of this Block.

Rows 11–20: With buff in place of royal and coffee in place of delft blue, rep rows 1–10 of this Block.

Rows 21–30: Rep rows 1–10 of this Block.

5TH BLOCK
Work same as 3rd Block.

6TH BLOCK
Work same as 2nd Block.

7TH BLOCK
Work same as 3rd Block.

STRIP B
MAKE 2.
FIRST BLOCK
Row 1: With ranch red, ch 29, sc in 2nd ch from hook and in each ch across, turn. *(28 sc)*

Row 2: Work row 3 of Pattern.

Row 3: With shocking pink, work row 1 of Pattern.

Row 4: Work row 3 of Pattern.

Rows 5 & 6: With ranch red, work rows 2 and 3 of Pattern.

Rows 7–10: Rep rows 3–6 of this Block.

Row 11: With coffee, work row 1 of Pattern.

Rows 12 & 13: Work row 2 of Pattern.

Row 14: Work row 3 of Pattern.

Rows 15 & 16: With claret, work rows 1 and 3 of Pattern.

Rows 17–20: Rep rows 11–14 of this Block.

Row 21: With ranch red, work row 1 of Pattern.

Rows 22–30: Rep rows 2–10 of this Block.

2ND BLOCK
Rows 1 & 2: With real teal, work rows 1 and 3 of Pattern.

Row 3: With hunter green, work row 1 of Pattern.

Row 4: Work row 3 of Pattern.

Rows 5 & 6: With real teal, work rows 2 and 3 of Pattern.

Rows 7–30: [Rep rows 3–6 of this Block consecutively] 6 times.

3RD BLOCK
Rows 1 & 2: With spring green, work rows 1 and 3 of Pattern.

Rows 3 & 4: With turqua, work rows 1 and 3 of Pattern.

Rows 5–8: Rep rows 1–4 of this Block.

Row 9: With magenta, work row 1 of Pattern.

Rows 10 & 11: Work row 2 of Pattern.

Row 12: Work row 3 of Pattern.

Row 13: With pumpkin, work row 1 of Pattern.

Rows 14–17: Work row 2 of Pattern.

Row 18: Work row 3 of Pattern.

Rows 19–22: Rep rows 9–12 of this Block.

Rows 23 & 24: With turqua, work rows 1 and 3 of Pattern.

Rows 25 & 26: With spring green, work rows 1 and 3 of Pattern.

Rows 27–30: Rep rows 23–26 of this Block.

4TH BLOCK
Work same as 2nd Block of this Strip.

5TH BLOCK
Row 1: With light coral, work row 1 of Pattern.

Rows 2–11: Work row 2 of Pattern.

Row 12: Work row 3 of Pattern.

Rows 13 & 14: With claret, work rows 1 and 3 of Pattern.

Rows 15 & 16: With coffee, work rows 1 and 3 of Pattern.

Rows 17 & 18: With claret, work rows 1 and 3 of Pattern.

Rows 19–30: Rep rows 1–12 of this Block.

6TH BLOCK
Work same as 2nd Block on this Strip.

7TH BLOCK
Row 1: With ranch red, work row 1 of Pattern.

Row 2: Work row 3 of Pattern.

Row 3: With shocking pink, work row 1 of Pattern.

Row 4: Work row 3 of Pattern.

Rows 5 & 6: With ranch red, work rows 2 and 3 of Pattern.

Rows 7–10: Rep rows 3–6 of this Block.

Row 11: With coffee, work row 1 of Pattern.

Rows 12 & 13: Work row 2 of Pattern.

Row 14: Work row 3 of Pattern.

Rows 15 & 16: With claret, work rows 1 and 3 of Pattern.

Rows 17–20: Rep rows 11–14 of this Block.

Row 21: With ranch red, work row 1 of Pattern.

Rows 22–30: Rep rows 2–10 of this Block.

STRIP C
FIRST BLOCK
Row 1: With hunter green, ch 29, sc in 2nd ch from hook and in each ch across, turn. *(28 sc)*

Row 2: Work row 3 of Pattern.

Row 3: With real teal, work row 1 of Pattern.

Row 4: Work row 3 of Pattern.

Rows 5 & 6: With hunter green, work rows 2 and 3 of Pattern.

Rows 7–30: [Rep rows 3–6 of this Block consecutively] 6 times.

2ND BLOCK
Row 1: With pumpkin, work row 1 of Pattern.

Row 2: Work row 3 of Pattern.

Rows 3 & 4: With light coral, work rows 1 and 3 of Pattern.

Rows 5–8: Rep rows 1–4 of this Block.

Rows 9 & 10: Rep rows 1 and 2 of this Block.

Row 11: With ranch red, work row 1 of Pattern.

Rows 12 & 13: Work row 2 of Pattern.

Row 14: Work row 3 of Pattern.

Rows 15 & 16: With claret, work rows 1 and 3 of Pattern.

Row 17: With ranch red, work row 1 of Pattern.

Rows 18 & 19: Work row 2 of Pattern.

Row 20: Work row 3 of Pattern.

Rows 21–30: Rep rows 1–10 of this Block.

3RD BLOCK

Rows 1 & 2: With hunter green, work rows 1 and 3 of Pattern.

Row 3: With real teal, work row 1 of Pattern.

Row 4: Work row 3 of Pattern.

Rows 5 & 6: With hunter green, work rows 2 and 3 of Pattern.

Rows 7–30: [Rep rows 3–6 of this Block consecutively] 6 times.

4TH BLOCK

Rows 1 & 2: With delft blue, work rows 1 and 3 of Pattern.

Rows 3 & 4: With turqua, work rows 1 and 3 of Pattern.

Rows 5–8: Rep rows 1–4 of this Block.

Rows 9 & 10: Rep rows 1 and 2 of this Block.

Rows 11 & 12: With pumpkin, work rows 1 and 3 of Pattern.

Rows 13 & 14: With shocking pink, work rows 1 and 3 of Pattern.

Rows 15–18: Rep rows 11–14 of this Block.

Rows 19 & 20: Rep rows 11 and 12 of this Block.

Rows 21–30: Rep rows 1–10 of this Block.

5TH BLOCK

Work same as 3rd Block on this Strip.

6TH BLOCK

Row 1: With ranch red, work row 1 of Pattern.

Row 2: Work row 3 of Pattern.

Rows 3 & 4: With claret, work rows 1 and 3 of Pattern.

Rows 5–8: Rep rows 1–4 of this Block.

Rows 9 & 10: Rep rows 1 and 2 of this Block.

Rows 11 & 12: With light coral, work rows 1 and 3 of Pattern.

Rows 13 & 14: With pumpkin, work rows 1 and 3 of Pattern.

Rows 15 & 16: With light coral, work rows 1 and 3 of Pattern.

Rows 17–20: Rep rows 13–16 of this Block.

Rows 21–30: Rep rows 1–10 of this Block.

7TH BLOCK

Work same as 3rd Block on this Strip.

FINISHING

Sew Strips tog with hunter green, matching Blocks in the following order: Strip A, Strip B, Strip C, Strip B and Strip A.

EDGING

Rnd 1: With RS facing, join hunter green with sc in any corner, 2 sc in same corner, evenly sp sc around so Afghan lies flat, with 3 sc in each corner, **join** (see Pattern Notes) in beg sc, turn.

Rnd 2: Ch 1, sc in each st around with 3 sc in each center corner st, join in beg sc, **do not turn.** Fasten off.

Rnd 3: Join shocking pink with sc in any st, ch 1, sk next st, [sc in next st, ch 1, sk next st] around, join in beg sc. Fasten off. ∎

Stitch Guide

For more complete information, visit **FreePatterns.com**

ABBREVIATIONS

beg	begin/begins/beginning
bpdc	back post double crochet
bpsc	back post single crochet
bptr	back post treble crochet
CC	contrasting color
ch(s)	chain(s)
ch-	refers to chain or space previously made (e.g., ch-1 space)
ch sp(s)	chain space(s)
cl(s)	cluster(s)
cm	centimeter(s)
dc	double crochet (singular/plural)
dc dec	double crochet 2 or more stitches together, as indicated
dec	decrease/decreases/decreasing
dtr	double treble crochet
ext	extended
fpdc	front post double crochet
fpsc	front post single crochet
fptr	front post treble crochet
g	gram(s)
hdc	half double crochet
hdc dec	half double crochet 2 or more stitches together, as indicated
inc	increase/increases/increasing
lp(s)	loop(s)
MC	main color
mm	millimeter(s)
oz	ounce(s)
pc	popcorn(s)
rem	remain/remains/remaining
rep(s)	repeat(s)
rnd(s)	round(s)
RS	right side
sc	single crochet (singular/plural)
sc dec	single crochet 2 or more stitches together, as indicated
sk	skip/skipped/skipping
sl st(s)	slip stitch(es)
sp(s)	space/spaces/spaced
st(s)	stitch(es)
tog	together
tr	treble crochet
trtr	triple treble
WS	wrong side
yd(s)	yard(s)
yo	yarn over

Chain—ch: Yo, pull through lp on hook.

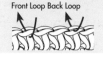

Slip stitch—sl st: Insert hook in st, pull through both lps on hook.

Single crochet—sc: Insert hook in st, yo, pull through st, yo, pull through both lps on hook.

Front post stitch—fp: Back post stitch—bp: When working post st, insert hook from right to left around post st on previous row.

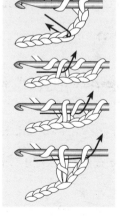

Back   Front

Post of Stitch

Front loop—front lp Back loop—back lp

Front Loop Back Loop

Half double crochet— hdc: Yo, insert hook in st, yo, pull through st, yo, pull through all 3 lps on hook.

Double crochet—dc: Yo, insert hook in st, yo, pull through st, [yo, pull through 2 lps] twice.

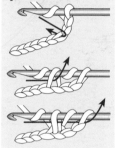

Double treble crochet—dtr: Yo 3 times, insert hook in st, yo, pull through st, [yo, pull through 2 lps] 4 times.

Change colors: Drop first color; with 2nd color, pull through last 2 lps of st.

Treble crochet—tr: Yo twice, insert hook in st, yo, pull through st, [yo, pull through 2 lps] 3 times.

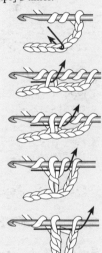

Treble crochet decrease (tr dec): Holding back last lp of each st, tr in each of the sts indicated, yo, pull through all lps on hook.

Example of 2-tr dec

Single crochet decrease (sc dec): (Insert hook, yo, draw lp through) in each of the sts indicated, yo, draw through all lps on hook.

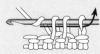

Example of 2-sc dec

Half double crochet decrease (hdc dec): (Yo, insert hook, yo, draw lp through) in each of the sts indicated, yo, draw through all lps on hook.

Example of 2-hdc dec

Double crochet decrease (dc dec): (Yo, insert hook, yo, draw loop through, draw through 2 lps on hook) in each of the sts indicated, yo, draw through all lps on hook.

Example of 2-dc dec

US		UK
sl st (slip stitch)	=	sc (single crochet)
sc (single crochet)	=	dc (double crochet)
hdc (half double crochet)	=	htr (half treble crochet)
dc (double crochet)	=	tr (treble crochet)
tr (treble crochet)	=	dtr (double treble crochet)
dtr (double treble crochet)	=	ttr (triple treble crochet)
skip	=	miss

Metric
Conversion
Charts

METRIC CONVERSIONS

yards	x	.9144	=	metres (m)
yards	x	91.44	=	centimetres (cm)
inches	x	2.54	=	centimetres (cm)
inches	x	25.40	=	millimetres (mm)
inches	x	.0254	=	metres (m)

centimetres	x	.3937	=	inches
metres	x	1.0936	=	yards

INCHES INTO MILLIMETRES & CENTIMETRES (Rounded off slightly)

inches	mm	cm	inches	cm	inches	cm	inches	cm
1/8	3	0.3	5	12.5	21	53.5	38	96.5
1/4	6	0.6	5 1/2	14	22	56	39	99
3/8	10	1	6	15	23	58.5	40	101.5
1/2	13	1.3	7	18	24	61	41	104
5/8	15	1.5	8	20.5	25	63.5	42	106.5
3/4	20	2	9	23	26	66	43	109
7/8	22	2.2	10	25.5	27	68.5	44	112
1	25	2.5	11	28	28	71	45	114.5
1 1/4	32	3.2	12	30.5	29	73.5	46	117
1 1/2	38	3.8	13	33	30	76	47	119.5
1 3/4	45	4.5	14	35.5	31	79	48	122
2	50	5	15	38	32	81.5	49	124.5
2 1/2	65	6.5	16	40.5	33	84	50	127
3	75	7.5	17	43	34	86.5		
3 1/2	90	9	18	46	35	89		
4	100	10	19	48.5	36	91.5		
4 1/2	115	11.5	20	51	37	94		

KNITTING NEEDLES CONVERSION CHART

Canada/U.S.	0	1	2	3	4	5	6	7	8	9	10	10½	11	13	15
Metric (mm)	2	2¼	2¾	3¼	3½	3¾	4	4½	5	5½	6	6½	8	9	10

CROCHET HOOKS CONVERSION CHART

Canada/U.S.	1/B	2/C	3/D	4/E	5/F	6/G	8/H	9/I	10/J	10½/K	N
Metric (mm)	2.25	2.75	3.25	3.5	3.75	4.25	5	5.5	6	6.5	9.0

Annie's Attic®

TOLL-FREE ORDER LINE or to request a free catalog (800) LV-ANNIE (800) 582-6643
Customer Service (800) AT-ANNIE (800) 282-6643, **Fax** (800) 882-6643
Visit AnniesAttic.com
We have made every effort to ensure the accuracy and completeness of these instructions.
We cannot, however, be responsible for human error, typographical mistakes or variations in individual work.

ISBN: 978-1-59635-265-0